THREE NOVELLAS

Contents

To My Wife

A TRUTH LOVER

Freedom: by definition, what has not been attained.

Today, which should have been a long stocktaking of freedom, found me instead becoming aware of new fetters, fetters which I am not yet able to define. It is probably to be desired, now that my student days are ending, that I should begin to keep a journal; one day free from obligations has already been enough for me to apprehend a creeping sluggishness on the move in my skull. All day I seem to have stood around torpidly, feeling disillusion eroding the light-headedness of the relief which came with the completion of exams. I had projected activities for this time: swimming at North Berwick, walking in the Pentlands, even lazing in my bed. In the event that I have done nothing but roam the streets of the city with Alan Bryce, as always when I have better things to do. Today I had a searching argument with Bryce. The subject, religion.

A fine June afternoon after finals, yet I felt disturbed. We drifted without direction, following schoolgirls for amusement; we could not be bothered talking much. Alan was in a sort of daze, I thought, whereas I felt fidgety and full of unease. My disturbance was accentuated by the balmy, slightly sweaty weather. I find heat physically uncomfortable; give me a cool, grey day when I can walk long distances by myself, fast but without sweating, and later read or just stand about in my room with a clear conscience. Such a day makes no demands upon one. I rather fear and dislike good weather; it oppresses me, I suppose, with the sense of the many opportunities it offers which somehow I always fail to take. Whatever activity I choose it seems the wrong one, and always I am sure I would have been happier elsewhere. And now that my life is to be my own at last I see that the same problem faces me permanently and on a much larger scale: faced with a riot of possibilities how shall I be able to choose between them, how determine upon any single form of action which will give shape to my outward life; how above all will I give a form to my obsessional resolve to life by the code of truth?

The coming divergence of our paths seemed to lie heavily on Alan and myself this afternoon. Perhaps that is why I tried to force certain things into the light: I was gritting my mind, too, feeling for a rough pathway which my feet might grip amid the deserts of my will. I seemed possessed by a purposeful negativism. We spoke desultorily of the future: I said that I would neither read nor write a thesis. "Perhaps I should have been a philosopher like you," I said, and Bryce replied that he only played at philosophy. This displeased me somewhat, his words rankled in me. He asked me how I intended to live, and I could answer only that something would doubtless emerge in time. It is rare for Bryce and myself to find each other irritating. I considered whether it was not the conscious viciousness which we have in common which had made us friends.

Bryce was eating out of a paper bag those boilings to which he is addicted. He told me once that he enjoyed taking a bagful into the National Library with him, where he would sit clacking them against his teeth and cracking them loudly to the fury of those around him. As we walked along he suddenly punted one of these sweets into the middle of the street, where it bounced on the roof of a car with a loud ping. I watched him with amusement, scuttling along beside me, a small sturdy nimble man, his expression deadpan but his mouth smiling faintly. He has always to bustle to keep up with my long strides, because of the shortness of his shanks. Our minds, though, are very similar. I was in a sour frame of mind, and experienced a perverse desire to provoke my friend. Progressing at one stage in the afternoon along a narrow stretch of pavement in the Canongate, we found our path partially blocked by the slow progress of an extremely bent old woman and by the actions of her walking-stick which splayed out at an angle of forty-five degrees to the pavement. "Jostle her into the gutter', suggested Bryce, and made as if to do so, but he dodged past her on his rugby player's toes. This small incident initiated a conversation which has much disturbed me. For we began to consider in our customary sardonic manner the desirability, from the economic and social standpoints, of the abolition of old folk by means of the painless destruction of all citizens over seventy years of age. 'I can see,' said Bryce, 'the psychological barriers against actual killing. We cannot expect such a radical degree of enlightenment to come quickly. May I suggest this solution: the employment by the state, on a subsistence or rather below subsistence diet, of all registered old folk in rough manual labour—as dustmen or stone breakers, say, or in pulling milk floats. This method would speedily accomplish our primary aims without any taint of moral stigma, and would also provide the economy with a large unskilled labour force with a high turnover, if no great degree of mobility.' I was in no mood, though, for our usual type of discourse, and my mind continued to worry away at some falsity in our friendship, so I added, rather brutally, 'And they'd get a Christian burial.' I glanced sideways at Alan, and saw the muscles hardening and freezing on his face.

We had it out then, giving vent to many opinions and emotions which we had long suppressed; and we brought into the open the source of the tension which had added to our intimacy the pleasure of an unspoken antagonism. I taxed him, first, with not appreciating the seriousness of his own humour. He had told me that he only played at philosophy: I suggested to him that he only played at life, also. When he replied it was as if he were repeating a memorised statement which had been long ago prepared; he did not speak parrot-wise, however but rather with an agonised emphasis. He had on his Brethern face.

'It's as if there were two parts of me,' he said, 'a warm part and a cold part. The warm part sees things your way, Duncan, it represents everything that my natural instincts dictate and besides it's my personal habit of mind, it's what my moral nature would probably demand that I should be if the cold part didn't exist. If the warm part of me were all of me my humour *would* be completely serious, I wouldn't be playing with life at all. But the cold part tells me that without any doubt all of this doesn't matter at all, that everything is settled and ordained for me in a particular way, and it therefore exerts a certain discipline, a restricting discipline perhaps, upon my natural personality.'

'And this cold influence, I take it, is your Christian conviction?' I asked him.

'Yes,' Bryce replied; then paused a moment and said, 'I wish you were a Christian, Duncan'. I noticed a threatened break in his voice, and felt embarrassed. At the same time I felt a strong necessity to counter him.

I said to him something like this: 'I wish I could say I wished the same. I've often in the past envied you the firm basis which your conviction gives you from which to criticise life. But I can't see why all this should reduce the seriousness of that criticism. You blanket all of your free personality, including your natural perceptions, under the phrase "the warm part of me", and you say that what comes out of it does not matter. Now to dismiss all that seems to me to be immoral. What of the validity of your perceptions, which you can experience as immediately as the heat of your body? You're just giving yourself licence for a relaxation of seriousness in the immediate conduct of your life. What only the warm part of you believes, is the truth to me. Yet you've often harangued me for making light of what's serious for others: just as I felt you freeze just now when I mentioned Christian burial.'

Alan had on his most sombre visage by now. 'I've often heard preachers say of unbelievers that though their outward mind resists the Gospel yet in their heart of hearts they know that they are wrong. But I don't think its universally true. I don't think it's the case with you.'

It seemed to me he was merely trying to persuade himself of this, and I did not know what to answer. I felt curiously disturbed, but also a little disgusted. I could not decide whether an element of mechanism was taking over in my friend. He seemed eager to pursue the matter. 'But to take you up on your point,' he continued, 'what makes you rely so heavily on what comes out of your own personality—your perceptions, your integrity and so on? I'm jealous of my integity too I think, but you're fanatical about yours.'

To this remark I felt a strong positive response: I realised its truth and I relished that truth. We were walking down the Mound at the time and I could see the New Town stretched below me in the sun, and between the buildings I could catch glimpses of the Fife hills, just visible through the haze. I swept my eyes from Corstorphine Hill to the Calton and felt suddenly in possession of my city, of the inheritance I knew was mine. A hard strength held me, and I felt convinced that the direction and embodiement of my will which I have been semi-consciously seeking for so many months were all but within my grasp.

'Certainly I rely upon anything which comes to me with the conviction of truth,' I said vehemently, 'you can't claim a monopoly of conviction, you know; nor, I think, of truth either.' I was dizzied by my certainty.

'And what's the source of the conviction that has no sanction outside your own mind?' he asked. 'It can have only one source, Duncan, your pride, it's as simple as that, the violence of your spiritual pride.'

I became somewhat pedantic in my own defence: 'As a philosopher, even a playtime philosopher,' I said, 'you surely won't assert that the sanction that can't be pointed to can have no existence.'

I saw then that we were out of the deep waters, we had wallowed into the shallows of half-seriousness; our friendship would be preserved, but somehow, again, a possibility had been missed. I don't feel yet in a position to comment on this long exchange: it wasn't without significance for me, certainly, but the exact nature of that significance—no, I can't unravel it yet. I remember I ended by making quite spontaneously a remark I had no intention of making, and the relationship of which to what had gone before eludes me: 'I'll admit the future is perhaps yours rather than mine.' Bryce gave me a curious look, as if he had been thinking the same thing himself but hadn't expected me to say it; so I felt obliged to add, 'I don't necessarily mean by that what you would mean.'

When we reached Princes Street I said with difficulty—for I have always hated addressing people by name—'I suppose I can't persuade you to a drink, Alan?'

'No, thanks,' he replied, 'other things apart, I'm late. So we come to the parting of the ways.'

Yes, perhaps.

This evening a curious succession of events in the Cromlech, which ended by my witnessing as act of great violence. It has precipitated a decision in me: I must record the whole sequence of events quite fully, I think.

It was another sultry day; I had slept too long in the morning and this had disoriented me somewhat so that by evening my mind was a sullen blank. I went to the Cromlech about six and settled down in my usual place with a pint and a steak pie, the latter more out of a sense of duty towards my stomach rather that from actual hunger. I knew I would be unable to relax until I had disposed of it, so I set to, though without much relish. The first mouthful proved to be tepid, which made me angry. It was not going to be my night, clearly. It was crowded; two businessmen came and propped their brutish rumps against my table. This sight, combined with the second unappetising mouthful of pie, acted upon my irritable nerves sufficiently to induce a retch-like spasm in my throat, and I had to push my plate away and stop eating. So I took a drink of beer and lit a cigarette, and lay back limply in my seat. After a bit, though, the familiar scene and the few kent faces which I didn't know well enough to have to acknowledge, gradually soothed me, and I began to be conscious of a more palpable sense of freedom than I had experienced since finishing the exams. An obscure but definite expectancy, too, was stirring in me: I felt that some direction was about to be indicated to me.

This mildly euphoric reverie was interrupted after a few minutes by the approach of an old man who was trying to persuade people to tip him in return for his clearing away empty glasses. He was a pitifully drab figure in a long belted raincoat of indeterminate colour, shaven and with a degenerate felt hat on his head. I watched his approach with angered trepidation, for I loathe being interrupted and imposed upon. The old beggar was working his way around the bar and would inevitably reach me in due course. Most people were treating him with a jocular tolerance, a few were even giving him coppers or sixpences. I had naturally not the slightest intention of doing either. My pint glass was still about a quarter full, and I could see the old man making to lift it.

'Leave that alone,' I said sharply. The beggar's hand was already on it, however, and he said, 'You want tae drink it up, sir?'

I shouted furiously 'Leave it alone, I said!' and grapped the glass away. The old man then offered me a filthy hand to shake, and blessed me. I ignored the proffered hand and the beggar stretched it out and patted me on the head; I struck out in rage and distaste, and the derelict moved off, saying 'God bless you, sir' significantly. I detest beggars who bless me, call me 'sir' and thank me for refusing them. I have only once, that I can remember, given money to a beggar. I had passed him sitting on a bench on the Mound, and walked on regardless of his 'Excuse me, sir'. After I had passed, though, I heard the man's voice shouting, with what seemed genuine desolation, 'Christ, what's the matter with me? Naebody'll answer me!' So I turned back and gave him a half-crown.

A former school acquaintance of mine had been watching this incident from a distance with evident amusement, and now he came over, bringing me a consolatory pint of heavy. He said I took things too seriously. 'The old brute,' I said, 'why the devil don't they put him off the premises?' He introduced me to a young man and girl who were with him. The girl was a vapid-looking tart who professed to be a state of distraction because half her clothes were in Paris and the other half in Rotterdam, and she hadn't a thing with her. When I was introduced to the young man as 'Duncan Straiton' he asked, 'Do you stick to the strait 'n narrow?' He was the type who comes up from London twice a year and gravitates to the Cromlech because it used to be his home during the six months between his leaving school and his departure for the southern fleshpots. His name was James Jardine and he was the essence of modish conventional smartness, with a face of complacent blonde friendliness. They all squeezed down beside me and the conversation flickered weakly for a time. When a group of workmen from the building site down the street came in to spend their Friday pay-packets, Jardine said, 'Well, well, well!' in a tone of mock outrage, and arched his eyebrows.

'The place is not what it was,' I said with heavy sarcasm. Jardine, however, took my remark at face value. 'Aha, I see you're a typical Edinburgh snob,' he said complacently, wagging a finger at me. I am ashamed to say that for a moment of weakness I experienced a faint glow of pleasure at the implied comradeship—I must be lonelier than I'd suspected; so that when my better nature asserted itself again I despised Jardine the more virulently.

The talk veered, inevitably, to the General Election which is supposed to be in the offing, and Jardine, who had proclaimed himself a Tory, leaned over to ask me how I intended to vote; for I had been silent and he clearly felt it to be his social duty to show me kindness by drawing me into the discussion. I replied shortly that I didn't intend to vote since there was no Nationalist candidate for my constituency. At this he pricked up his ears with the air of one who has scented a vaguely controversial topic which he is confident he can handle. Subsequently he furnished much evidence of obtuseness and vacuity, adopting a conciliatory tone which merely succeeded in rendering him patronising. I was unco-operative and disinclined to argue. He spoke a little of the modern world, his modern world. At this he began to bluster, spoke with mordant sarcasm of a nation of poets, and turned away to pester someone on the other side of the bar. My school friend had already moved off, and this left me sitting alone beside Jardine's girl friend. She began trying to engage me in conversation, asking me what I did for a living, making disparaging remarks about Jardine, and even resorting to the weather in the face of a barrier of grunts and monosyllables from myself. My silence was initially of necessity, for I am chronically tongue-tied with women and particularly with women of this sort, and for a time I struggled vainly to think of bright replies. After a minute of two however I reflected that there was nothing to be gained by talking to her and that I had no desire to do so anyway, so I continued to grunt as a matter of policy. The girl was evidently concerned mainly with inducing a state of jealousy in Jardine who was ignoring her completely.

'I sometimes wonder why he bothers to take me out at all,' she said plaintively.

'H'm,' I replied politely. The girl gave up.

I began to think about leaving, for my solitude had been disturbed and I found the present situation embarrassing. I thought how pleasant it would be to walk down the hill to my flat through the quiet streets in the approaching cool of the evening. The strange feeling of expectancy which I had experienced earlier had not left me, however, so I continued to sit on, watching the party of labourers who were becoming noisy as they put away their whiskies and beers. They were clearly enjoying themselves and I felt a certain admiration for their gusto

and their lack of apology for themselves: a refreshing contrast
to myself. A sentimental thought, perhaps.

In a moment Jardine was making his way back from the far
side of the bar; his path was blocked by a knot of labourers and
I could see him excusing himself and asking to be let through.
They paid no attention; their backs were to him and quite
possibly they had not heard or noticed him. A look of insulted
irritation came over his face and he began to push his way
rudely through the middle of them. One of them had a fullish
pint glass in his hand: the young man jolted it and beer slopped
down the workman's shirt. The latter, a stocky hirsute man with
a great broad face and stiff brush-like hair rooted from about a
couple of inches above his eyes, turned round towards Jardine
at first with an utterly blank blank look, his reactions slowed and
numbed by many pints and nips. Unhappily for the young man
something in his face must have struck at the workman's mind
so that it cracked and disintegrated, and he was left purely in
the control of his physical instincts. His attitudes reminded me
of the blind and dogged violence of the Frankenstein monster.
With his left hand the man turned Jardine and shoved his
back against the bar, and with his right drove the open end of
the beer glass carefully into the middle of his face. The glass
cracked and split, beer cascaded over Jardine's fashionable
shirt and blood began to exude over his face. Deliberately and
doggedly the man had turned the broken glass in the helpless
face; he let it go and dropped it, and stook blankly, his own
fingers dripping. The scene, indeed the whole incident, was
unbelievably and deplorably theatrical.

Silence had overtaken all those who could see, but Jardine
had not screamed, and pockets of conversation from secluded
corners where the event had not yet penetrated added to the
pervasive unreality of the moment. Jardine was leaning on the
bar with his face in his hands; gurgling sounds came from him
and blood was trickling between his fingers and over his signet
ring. I was aware of the young man's feet in their polished
shoes and of his modish trouser-legs, and of how the feet and

legs were oddly quiet and undisturbed by the catastrophe which had overtaken the other extremity of the body to which they belonged: the idea produced an odd pity in me, and I though how a few minutes earlier Jardine had been an amiable young man discussing politics. These thoughts occupied a matter of seconds, then the girl became hysterical, a barmaid rushed for the phone, and chaos was come in the bar.

I remained sitting quietly in an almost catatonic state. Violence, it seemed, was so much a part of the landscape of my own mind that its physical actuality made little immediate impression upon me. I felt little sense of horror, only a persistence of the slightly nauseating pity summoned up in me by Jardine's legs. The victim had been led to a table where he was invisible behind a gabbling crowd, but his groans had become very audible. The assailant still appeared stunned; his workmates were unobtrusively keeping watch on him with the help of a barman, but he did not seem likely to make any attempt at escape, and just gazed sadly at his cut finger. The girl stood sobbing loudly but tearlessly—no one paid her much attention.

My consciousness began to latch onto a significance for me in the scene which I had witnessed, a significance which I knew I must approach with care. A powerful exhilaration buoyed me up so that I sat there in the Cromlech with what must have been a crazy-looking grin on my face. I cannot yet justify intellectually the seed which began to grow in my mind as I sat in on that grotesque situation; but by the time the police arrived I knew beyond doubt that eventually, when I am called upon to give evidence against the labourer, I must refuse.

For two or three days I have been trying to establish to my own satisfaction why I made that decision the other night, which I have now come to think of as irrevocable, and whose consequences, once it has been put into effect, will never depart from me throughout my life (that much I know). To begin with I reasoned thus: I should trust my instinctive preference for the assailant over the victim, regarded simply as individuals: did it not show that at some level the workman was profoundly in the right? I could well understand how such an action was possible; indeed there seemed something almost heroic in that unequivocal surrender to the passion of the moment. Was it very different, after all, from the blow which I myself had struck that beggar half an hour before—was it not an honest expression of emotion such as only self-conciousness prevented many people from indulging in almost daily? The man had been right in feeling as he did, and he had acted only as he felt.

I have had to admit to myself, however, that these rationalised arguments about the inner ethics of the culprit's action go no more than skin deep, that indeed they are essentially immoral, because dishonest. Nor is it my extremely strong prejudice against the law, on this occasion, which is influencing me to act in this way. No, my decision is concerned not with justice but with will, not with the rights of either of the parties involved but with myself alone. In short its nature is perverse and arbitrary from any objective viewpoint. I have leapt at the first available opportunity of committing myself to a decisive act of will, a commitment to a dominant idea which will both set me apart from the multitude and determine my future. By defying the law I hope to make the acquaintance of my own nature, discover the truth through the suffering which this perverse commitment will entail. And already I find myself faced with the first question. How many things have I already said and done in the name of Truth which were instead nothing but assertions of my own will?

Alan Bryce is no doubt right. Within the spiral staircase of my own ego I am imprisoned. Thither I have beaten my retreat. Only once did I stop briefly at a slit of a window and catch a glimpse of the sun shining upon an indistinct landscape. But when I felt that warmth on my face I became afraid of sunstroke, so I turned away and ascended once more grimly through the chill, round and round that immobile centre-post.

My first love, Christine, was that narrow window. She remains somewhere within me to dog my dreams from time to time, a pervasive symbol of my failure, the type of all my lost and squandered opportunities of the life upon which I wilfully turned my back. Thus I have been faithful, after my fashion, faithful that is after the fashion of death. But the poses I have struck! This I wrote to her three years ago: 'For me our happiness was merely an interlude in a more rigorous life, I was never intended for the permanence of such an experience, I was destined for a starker vision than our dream. This truth is older than my youth and childhood, older than my conception, and I have had no choice but to be faithful to that truth.' What I was really talking about was my own stupidity and stubbornness, yet I have built upon this false and sentimental pose. For five years I have been alone and self-sufficient, I have loved no woman and approached none, fearing and shunning human contact, and instead I have dedicated myself to a harsh vision, developing everything in myself that is hard, chilly and reticent. And now these weapons of self-defence are eating me up.

Last night I dreamt that I lay in bed with Christine beside me, and I woke up hugging my scarecrow shoulders in my crossed arms as I might a lover, groaning in the barrenness of the sudden dissolution of my bliss. 'I am a man naturally intended for the most simple forms of happiness,' I said aloud, still half asleep—and was startled into wakefulness by an awareness of my own capacity for self-dramatisation.

How admirably I have co-operated with the law thus far in the affair! There's no telling how many police notebooks and files my statement now graces. The Procurator Fiscal, too, with his precognition, he couldn't have found in me any cause for complaint. Jardine lost an eye, it seems, and suffered scarring that will be permanent; and I felt truly sorry, and regretful, for a time, that I would be unable to play my part in the process of justice. Not that justice will not be done, as the world sees it, for other witnesses are not lacking. But now the time has come when my co-operation must cease; for I am cited to appear as a witness in the High Court two days from now. I must go for a time where they cannot lay hands on me: I think I shall follow the lure of foreign places, of obscure sensualities. A life of freedom seems about to open up before me for a time. Since it is now towards the end of July it will probably be too hot for me on the continent; but doubtless I can put up with it. What alternative have I left myself, in fact? Tomorrow I must pack my bags.

Meanwhile, a fable.

Once a long time ago, but also a long time after it had been scientifically proven, and generally accepted by the world at large, that the earth was a sphere which revolved round the sun, there was a man who persisted in believing that the earth was flat. It is not possible to say why, for the earth's rotundity cannot conceivably have been damaging to him, but it had become absolutely essential to his peace of mind that this belief should not be disturbed. Though in other respects he was a not unreasonable man, on this one point he stood steadfast and would not be moved. It was of no possible use attempting to alter this man's conviction by the presentation of objective evidence, no matter how compelling; he refused absolutely to accept any such, for he was possessed of a deeper knowledge, and this he was determined (obliged, he said) to assert even if he might appear arrogant in doing so. His friends did argue with him, of course: they could not simply have let the matter pass without making some effort in this direction. But it was the Age of Freedom of Conscience, and he would invariably reply,'Certainly you have that right': but on the other hand it was also the Age of Reason, and they were constrained to add, 'But your freedom to hold such an opinion is not in any way a guarantee of its objective validity.' The man knew he could not really counter this argument, but because it was the Age of Faith he felt justified in ignoring it. And that it should have been at one and the same time the Age of all these estimable virtues is by no means a contradiction.

To give this man his small due, he was loyally enough dedicated to his own vision: and though he would not accept the proofs offered against him by others, he saw no reason why they should not have to accept any evidence collected by him in support of his belief. So being a fairly rich man, he eventually determined to equip a ship and organise an expedition to establish his point. And off he sailed towards the horizon, quite prepared to drop off the edge of the world if necessary. The captain and crew whom he had hired knew very well of course that he was a crank, but what did they care? To circle the globe was not such an undertaking as it once had been, and they were being handsomely paid for doing it. It was a long slow voyage, interminably slow, and it was not until they were about three-quarters of the way round that it was suddenly borne in upon the man, in a moment of hideous conversation, that they were going to arrive back at the point they had started from. A great weariness had overtaken him: perhaps it was due to the unaccustomed rigours of the voyage, or to his terrible loneliness and the brooding hours he spent alone in his cabin, or to seasick days and bad dreams at night, or just to a sense of the horror of going on and on without end; but his will could suddenly withstand the onslaught of the truth no longer. He had been stretched too long upon the rack of his desire. And now he could feel nothing but the shock of his own betrayal of the truth, his truth, which he had always believed in. He felt himself, now that he had discovered the objective truth, to be a traitor who did not deserve to live. To make amends he must do what was in his power to salvage the honour of his old vision. So he ordered the ship to be turned round; this nearly provoked a mutiny but he flexed his will once more, and back they sailed the way they had come: an appalling, exhausting voyage it was. When he returned home he found himself something between a laughing-stock and a scandal: but he held his head up high. 'We had to turn back,' he told his friends, 'otherwise, who knows, we might have sailed on for ever. The earth may after all have no edge, I have never claimed that to be flat it must necessarily have an edge. Every day we sailed on would have meant further to come back—I couldn't do that to my sailors; many lives would have been lost if we had gone on. But there is no doubt at all of this: my point has been proved, the earth is most certainly not round. I can scarcely consider my expedition a failure when it has so gloriously vindicated the truth.' His friends could only shake their heads—the man was becoming a tiresome bore. 'All right,' they said, 'have it your own way. The earth is flat, as flat as a pancake, let's leave it at that!' Only then did the man feel free to go quietly out into the night and shoot himself.

But I do not think that I am ready yet to believe this fable.

Paris: a quiet hotel of too high a quality for my resources; and I have been here a week. In foreign places I need comfort to sustain my confidence. I have had little joy here so far. Every day I walk many miles in the sulty heat through the streets and parks of the city; it is a dead time in Paris and I feel exiled to the fringes of life. Everywhere I go I sense possibilities to which I am not admitted, in particular I am tortured and worn out by a lust which I have found no means of assuaging. Female images burden my brain, and my body aches with its failure to encompass them. Late in the afternoon I return to this room, dusty, sweaty and exhausted, and lie prone on the bed trying to summon up the energy to arrange for my daily bath—a major undertaking in this hotel. The chambermaids think me mad, possibly rightly, because of my passionate dedication to bodily cleanliness. After bathing I put on my lightweight suit and make my way to some restaurant where I eat expensively by myself and drink too much wine. Then I walk again, miles more. The air is never as cool as I think at first. I keep hoping for some romantic encounter, but none takes place, for I haven't the courage to let it. Midnight finds me always lying in this stuffy room once more, too tired to undress, firmly believing that something interesting and pleasant is going to happen to me tomorrow. Sometimes I go to sleep with my clothes on, then wake up feeling ghastly early in the morning, have to struggle out of them and arrange them carefully on a chair to air by the open window. Only then can I crawl thankfully between the cool but lonely sheets. Thus it goes: a dismal enough sort of freedom.

This morning I interrupted my wanderings as usual to have a beer at a pavement café: it is the thing to do in Paris and besides, I like beer. No sooner had the words 'Une bière, s'il vous plait' passed my lips than I heard a voice behind me congratulating me, on this slender evidence, on the quality of my French. I turned round to see a heavy, red-faced little man with a crew-cut who introduced himself as 'Guy Lozelle'. He was a French Canadian, he explained, and he asked if he might join me. There seemed to be no alternative to this proposal which would not have involved an embarrassment acuter than the nuisance of having to accept it, and after all I had scarcely spoken for more than a week beyond the cursory please's and thank you's necessary to maintain existence. So I said 'By all means.' M. Lozelle, it seemed, was a college instructor in engineering who had been everywhere and seen or done everything in the sexual encyclopaedia, and it appeared to be his mission in life to make the facts known to the world. Since I became bored with extreme rapidity by his accounts of promiscuity in Afghanistan, I decided to do some talking myself. I am after all far too good a listener for my own good. I wanted to test out some philosophico-religious ideas I have been toying with for the last few days, so I deflected the course of the conversation mercilessly to this end, and opened up brashly, and with this kind of stiff formality:

'Great men,' I said, 'can be divided into three principal categories: the man of action, the artist, and the seer or saint. Each has his own valid function and type of success. The man of action is he whose fruitfulness springs from human integration, he is ordered in his psyche because he lives below the level of metaphysical considerations. But for the second group, the contradictions of the human state constitute an obsession: they are eternally at war with themselves because they seek to find and express the relation of finite to infinite. So artistic success is gained always at the expense of human failure and unhappiness—the solution of the artist's problem would involve his death as an artist. Yet the artist's only escape is to abandon insight in favour of love, to join the ranks of the third group, the saints, who seek not to understand human life but to transcend it.'

The Canadian had listened to this dismal peroration with a considerable degree of attentiveness, which made me at once regret its crudity the more. After I had fallen silent Lozelle looked distant and preoccupied for a while, and kept tapping the rim of his beer glass against his teeth as if trying to crystallise something in his mind. Finally he began to talk again, distantly at first but then vehemently.

'I was interested in what you said about the man of action. There was a guy I knew once whom I still think of as the epitome of the type—the absolute man of action. I knew him when I was, oh, a good deal younger than you are now. It would be useless for me to try to describe to you the pure vitality of the man. I never knew him well but it was clear to me at once—and I may say this was a rare thing in the milieu in which we lived—that he didn't have a vulgar soul, if that's the way to put it. He was what they used to call in the old days, in that much hackneyed but maybe not altogether meaningless phrase, "a born leader of men". Not the type the phrase might lead you to expect, though: he was intelligent for a start, and I'd say an exception to what you said about the "integrated psyche" of the man of action—he wasn't happy. From the first time I saw him I judged that he had what the vulgar call "class" or "star quality". He was a kind of genius of action, I guess. I'm not altogether sure I liked him, though, and I'm certain he didn't like me. No, I never really got to know him. A good thing, probably. I hoped a great deal for that guy, as for myself, and now that all my own hopes have come to nothing, I like to continue to think that at least I may not have been wrong about him.'

I was really rather moved by what the Canadian had told me, but I was too haughty at that moment to admit it to myself, partly because I had an unpleasant feeling that Lozelle's contribution to the conversation had been of greater value than my own; so to convince myself of the man's cheapness and demerit I said internally, What a vulgar and tasteless fool, thus sentimentally to rationalise the homosexual passion of his adolescence.

Nonetheless, something of what I had heard must have struck a chord in my own mind, for the man of whom Lozelle had spoken reminded me in some way of that strange man Scrines, a distant relative I think of the girl Paula on whom I used to cast lascivious eyes (no more than eyes, alas). I felt in him at once, the first time I met him, an intangible but distinct hostility to myself. Scrines is a dark, hard, shortish young man with features of a surpassing strength and sharpness, and tense pale eyes ever on guard to repel any attempt at intimacy. He is all reticence and restraint, jealousy preserving that core of brutal integrity of which he is composed. He seldom speaks, and when he does it is with a harsh, blunt directness and in unlovely grating tones. He cannot be ignored, though. He is the personification of a highly developed will, a pure immalleable centre largely stripped of its humanity and cultured, perhaps, as an antidote to some deep and lasting hurt. He is a man whose belief in himself holds him like a vice, and for that reason he can achieve almost anything which he desires. A strong current of mingled attraction and dislike runs between us: we are strongly aware of each other's presence, but keep up a pretense of not showing it, Scrines maintaining a cold aloofness and myself feigning casualness and indifference. The truth of the matter is that I see in the whole character of Scrines a reflection of my own will which I keep closely concealed from the public gaze; in Scrines the will is bore core and surface, a raw animal thing exposed candidly for all to see.

Enough digression, however, for I have a most curious incident to record. The mood of intense concentration which our odd conversation had engendered in both us us soon slackened, and when we were eating ham rolls of rock-like French bread and drinking coffee, the Canadian invited me to come up to his hotel room and have a glass of whisky with him. I had little better to do, so we made our way to a cheap hotel in one of the narrow streets near the Rue de l'Opera. I soon had occasion to regret my naivety, for as soon as we reached the hotel it became clear that Lozelle had homosexual designs upon his guest. I now remembered too late that he had told me that I would get on in life because I was kinda handsome; besides, the man of action should have made me beware. I resent homosexuals for much the same reason that I resent beggars—their propensity for imposing their unwanted selves upon one. Lozelle began by turning the key in the lock (the chambermaids were always coming in without knocking, he said): and by drawing the curtains, against the glare of the midday sun. Then he produced the bottle of whisky and poured out generous measures into two tumblers. I drank mine down quickly to steady myself, for I was very frightened; and took hold of the bottle. The Canadian seemed pleased by this, and pressed me to take a swig. He professed to be suffering from the heat, and taking off his jacket and loosening his tie, he lay down on the bed with his shoes on. Without his jacket he appeared obscenely fleshy, but he seemed dangerously strong at the same time. Reddish hair peeped out of his white nylon shirt where he had opened some buttons. Even the most casual contact with his loathsome body would have sickened me, so I was close to panic.

'I'll have to be getting back to my own hotel,' I said, 'I've got some letters to write, and I'm very tired.'

'That's all right,' said the Canadian amiably, 'you can lie

down right here,' and patted the other half of the narrow bed on which he was lying.

The blatancy of this suggestion tempered my fear with a most needful anger, so, still holding the whisky bottle, I positioned myself within easy range of the door, took a swig, and grinned encouragingly at Lozelle. The man clearly thought the matter was all but decided, as indeed it was. I unlocked the door, saying, 'Thanks for the drink, friend', opened it, and tossed the bottle of whisky towards the basin in the corner of the room opposite me. I was out and shutting the door behind me when the crash came. I walked to the end of the corridor then plunged six steps at a time down the stairs, and ran laughing through the streets of Paris back to my own hotel.

This afternoon I was buoyed up by elation at the way in which I had defeated the homosexual, but now it seems to me on reflection a cruel little incident, sordid and vicious on both sides. I am afraid that it has soured me still further against the city, and now I shall fear to go out in the streets in case I should meet the man by chance. Ah well, I was getting tired of Paris anyway. Perhaps before long I shall move on.

So, already I am disillusioned with travel and freedom, I know that I cannot find what I am looking for this way. I rush through and away from experience at a rate of knots, driven on from place to place by my unhappiness which I carry always within me; a bit like Milton's Satan, but somewhat more ridiculous. Without a solid haven behind me I can get to grips with nothing, and always I find myself packing up again and setting off longingly for somewhere else—it is an old failing, this nervy restlessness, my enthusiasm for new enterprises waxes and wanes at least as quickly as the moon. I lack entirely the knack of participating easily in the life of the place where I find myself, and as a sentimental journeyer I am destined, it seems to be an ignominious failure. No *place* can make me happy, that is now quite apparent to me. Nor can I be made a great exile, even, for the concept of exile presupposes a homeland, somewhere in the realms of the attainable; and the past alone is now truly our homeland.

Here, the conditions of my life are wretched. The streets of Zürich were unusually quick to blister my feet when I first arrived. I needed a job and I needed somewhere to live, and neither was easy to come by. This was the sort of situation which most unsettles me, and the aching glare of the sun, too, left me dazed and dumb, so that I could not be bothered and found myself shirking the simple acts which would readily have alleviated my plight. Even going to an estate agent's to enquire about a room was an intolerable and exhausting effort. Somehow I did it though, after a two days' hesitation, and was jolted far out into the suburbs in a feverish tram, to be deposited at the end of a long street of cheap concrete apartment buildings. After walking a long way down the street I found the number I wanted and the door was opened by a fat motherly figure, the malice of whose eyes was shielded from me, until it was too late, by her twinking glasses. Our discussion of terms was hampered by my rudimentary school German, for the matron was strictly monolingual and surprised, besides they do not teach Swiss dialect in 'English' schools. I have never been a man for haggling, though—I seldom look at more than one of anything I want to acquire, whether it is a jacket, a car or lodging—so our business was soon completed. The matron evidently felt that some polite discourse was now in order, and told me that she liked the Scots people—she had met many at religious conferences. I understood the word 'religiös'? She was anxious on this point, and my heart sank. Only then did I take in fully the pious pictures, pamphlets and prayer-books and other tokens of devotion which littered the dismal living-room. I wished devoutly that I had not agreed to take the room, but it was too late, I was not up to the task of changing my mind at that stage. So I went back to my hotel, collected my luggage, and returned to the lodgings.

When I got back I found that a pamphlet entitled 'Ich komme bald' had been placed on my bedside table. I stowed it away under my suitcases to help me avoid the temptation of opening it casually and beginning to read. I did not wish to risk being further disturbed at this juncture. To the same end I exaggerated my incapacity to carry on an intelligible conversation in my landlady's tongue, hoping thus to forestall any possible attempts at conversion.

The surroundings are oppressive, and I soon discovered that my residence here is to be hedged about by sundry paltry rules the imparting of which by the landlady I have pretended to understand imperfectly. There is an elaborate system of double-locking the front door, for instance, neglect of which appears to rank as a sin of the deepest dye. Then there is a plastic bag which has to be kept tied for eternity over the spout of the cold tap, against its scarcely perceptible dripping, the rate of which I estimate at perhaps one drip every two minutes. After use (one franc) the bath has not only to be cleaned but also thoroughly dried. I have always prided myself on my fastidiousness but I am not in Frau Herzog's class. Worst of all I received, the first morning after moving in, a severe reprimand for washing after nine in the evening. I had disturbed Frau Herzog's raucous slumbers with my dutiful splashings, it seems, for she is in the habit of retiring very early to rest her back, with which, the Lord be praised, she suffers tortures.

In spite of these conditions I felt that, having installed myself in the lodgings, I should make at any rate a token attempt to obtain some work; my money, indeed, was running dangerously low. So I roused myself sufficiently to acquire a part-time job teaching in a school of English which pays me reasonably well and leaves me with many free hours. This has involved me in days of floundering angrily among the regulations for work permits, of destroying my feet trailing between town-halls, consulates, police stations and other official addresses, sweating ceaselessly in the endless heat but quite unable to train myself to walk more slowly. And the work, since it has begun, I have found scarcely tolerable: my pupils, whose interest in English is for the most part strictly commercial, tend towards stupidity, and I myself am proving a bad and impatient teacher. I am able to carry on only by refusing to think about the work at any time except when I am in the classroom, but since I have to take classes in the early evening on several days of the week, I find relaxation in the afternoons extremely difficult. The lodgings are a perpetual bane, for the exchanges of smiles and bows and stilted courtesies between the landlady and myself have done nothing to modify the plenitude of unexpressed antagonism which from the outset has marked our relationship. In the evening Frau Herzog seems always to have visitors, representatives perhaps of some religious sect, whom I never actually see but whose voices I can hear rising and falling monotonously and insidiously, enquiring and commenting, I am sure, on the unsound lodger lying next door on his unredeemed bed surrounded by his pagan books. None of this makes for the carefree heart.

But this, of course, is only a period of waiting for me, in terms of activities which the world recognises. I am marking time while I grow towards the full readiness to undertake my duty, to act decisively in accordance with my beliefs. It is a time in fact of invisible work. There are few people who can understand the nature of invisible work, the work of the spirit; but it is hard, brutal, constant and comprehensive work all the same. Its fruits are not immediately apparent, nor clearly apprehensible when they become so, and for this reason, and because it is materially unproductive, it is generally scorned and slighted; but without this invisible work nothing of any importance can be achieved. Its claims upon the individual are boundless; we must be prepared to lay down our happiness for the truth which we would make; and it can render our outward lives not only miserable, but ridiculous as well. So, while I wander aimlessly about Europe, the idle subject of a drab picaresque farce, I am nonetheless, invisibly, working.

Can there be something sympathetic about my face, I wonder? It seems almost impossible for me to settle myself quietly in a public place without someone coming and interrupting me and engaging me in conversation, when my only desire is to be left in peace to my own thoughts. It is said that cats have a curious instinctive tendency to foist themselves upon people who dislike them, and I have had very much the same experience with human beings. Two evenings ago it happened to me again. I had had an exhausting session at the school and afterwards I went to a restaurant just across the street and sat down to a large ham steak with 'pommes frites', and drank several glasses of the fine, pale-coloured beer they have on draught here. When I had finished eating I began to read the English-language newspaper which I had bought, mainly out of a sense of obligation; this proved to be my undoing. For I was still on the front page when a young man of about my own age, whom I had noticed earlier leafing through a sheaf of small typewritten papers on which he was making occasional corrections in red ink, came over with a friendly manner towards my table. He had a dark complexion with rather fleshy and red lips, and his first words confirmed my impression that he was an American.

'I hope you don't mind my bothering you,' he said,'but am I glad to find a guy that can speak the language!'

'Not at all,' I replied, 'please sit down.'

He held out his hand. 'Let me introduce myself. I have a difficult name to remember: it's rather a lovely Italian name: Benedict Parimalvoni.'

'How do you do, I'm Duncan Straiton,' I said, and he sat down.

I bought him a beer and we talked for a few minutes about this and that. He was a college graduate, he said, filling in time in Europe while waiting to be drafted for military service. He asked me about myself, too, but his interest was clearly only formal, for his attention kept reverting to the sheaf of papers which he had brought over with him and which he now fingered as they lay in his lap. He was clearly awaiting an opportunity to bring them into the conversation, whatever they might be, but was finding difficulty in steering things the right way. I would willingly have helped him, had I known what they were, for I had no active dislike of the man. Finally a lull in the talk gave him the chance to ask me: 'I wonder whether perhaps you have any interest in poetry?' I had to admit that I had.

The bundle of papers was now shyly brought into view: Benedict Parimalvoni fondled them contemplatively, lovingly.

'I have just been preparing this little book of poems for publication,' he said softly, 'and perhaps I can risk boring you by letting you see them. They are very simple little verses, but quite new in their intentions and methods, I believe. They are children's poems, really, designed to be read by the mother to the child at her knee. The child in the poems asks the mother questions as he would in life, as children do, questions about life and death and birth and about all the things he sees around him in his daily existence; and the mother tries to answer him without talking down to him, but with simplicity, honesty and faith.'

He paused and cast a dark, baleful look at me. 'I am trying in these poems to regain something intangible which seems to be missing in modern life,' he said, 'call it what you will. Perhaps, in a sense, I am asking the questions the child asks. Something has to be held onto, I think, when we are living in the imminence of nuclear apocalypse. Maybe you feel the same way yourself.' His soft, fruity, lugubrious face made me want to laugh.

'At present,' I replied, tapping the newspaper in front of me, 'I am much more concerned by this iniquitous trade in tortoises.'

The American was uncertain how to take this, so I continued to look at him solemnly, and he began to nod his head vehemently.

'I stand by the sacredness of all living things, of course,' he assured me. 'You will see that from these poems. A friend of my father's is a publisher and he thinks very highly of them—he plans to bring them out in a little volume later this year. But I will let you judge for yourself.'

I took the sacred bundle and began with considerable embarrassment to read. They proved to be the most lamentable codswallop, sickly and fushionless beyond relief. The detestable child kept asking questions like 'What makes the sun rise, mother?' and she would answer, 'He who makes the birds sing, that same One makes the sun rise, Little One.' Throughout the sequence, in the face of a steady stream of precocious or imbecile questions, the mother persisted in addressing the tiresome brat as 'Little One.' I had quickly to decide whether honesty or kindness would be more valuable in this case, and felt naturally disposed towards honesty. However, the beer had put me in a mellow and indulgent mood, and I settled eventually for a non-committal comment on the imagery.

'Yes,' said Benedict eagerly, 'I must admit myself that I find them rather remarkable.'

Apart from the fact that his remark was a *non sequitur* from mine, which greatly irritated me, it was that 'rather' which made me see red and forget my good resolution about charity. If the silly fellow insisted in thinking his poems remarkable, why not go the whole hog and say so unequivocally? Why "rather remarkable"?

'My general impression, however,' I said, 'is that you must have been high on rose-hip syrup when you wrote this stuff. If my mother had read me anything like this when I stood at her knee, I'd have thrown up over it.'

Benedict Parimalvoni got up from his chair and with shaking fingers fumbled to arrange the little rectangles of typescript. His lips started to quiver and I feared that he was about to burst into tears. He put the poems carefully in the inside pocket of his jacket and with a trembling voice said, 'You have the mind of a cruel and narrow Puritan.' Then he gave me a still little half-bow from the waist, turned, and walked out of the restaurant, his face still working.

This incident had an effect on me very similar to that which

33

had attended my encounter with M. Lozelle, and which had precipitated my departure from Paris. It left me feeling once again sick at myself and at life, and immediately decided me on leaving Zurich as soon as possible. The protracted heat-wave had anyway been persuading me to this move for a week or more; it was almost unprecedented, I was told, for such heat to persist here so late in September. I always have the misfortune to find myself tormented by unprecedented weather conditions, wherever I go—it is a jinx, I'm convinced. Nor was there any way to escape this heat, for my detestation of my lodgings always kept me out almost all day. This overpowering stifling heat, this impossibility of escape, filled me with panic. Standing amid the petrol fumes of street corners and walking along the angles of buildings whose sheer concrete mercilessly deflected upon me the assaults of the afternoon sun, I found myself out of humour with those who found beneficient this massive token of their debtorship. I looked up with envy at the windows of the air-conditioned office blocks in which white shirts towered above the roar of the traffic and the brutal glare of the pavements. Even the women did not seem to wilt, only I wilted in that unnatural heat. The only place where I could find some refuge was the cool beer-house where I would sit for hours in a sort of dwalm of suspension from the life around me. It was here that it first struck me how desirable a haven was the security and coolness of a prison cell in my native land—and one which I had every chance of attaining. By now, after all, a warrant for my arrest might have been issued at home. I became eager once more to embrace my fate, just because I so coveted this sensuous consummation of a cool prison cell. I must do everything in my power to achieve it. What a prospect of peace, of relaxation, of solitude (if only I could get a single cell!). No responsibilities, no decisions to be made, no new places to have to travel to or work to be done, nobody to importune me, and all this in the worthy cause of self-determination! So here I am now, speeding across France in a wagon-lit, writing this journal with difficulty because of the swaying and jerking of the train, as excited as if I were being borne to the arms of a lover.

I parted with Frau Herzog as I had lived with her—in rancour. My suspicions of her hopes of converting me had been largely confirmed over the past weeks by various remarks and actions of hers, and recently she has started wooing me with gifts of oranges and grapes. I am not to be bought, however. I determined to leave with a flourish. By fortune she was to be away in the country all day yesterday visiting her son, so I determined to fix this as the day of my departure, and to decamp without giving her any warning. I had paid my rent for the next fortnight in advance, so my conscience on that score was clear, but for good measure I left on my bedside table a neat pile of eleven francs for ten days' worth of baths owed to the matron. Then I got out the pamphlet 'Ich komme bald', wrote on the cover, 'Und ich gehe bald, du alte Kuh', and laid it beside the coins, together with a copy of 'The Group' by Mary McCarthy, which I had bought for some train journey and had no further use for. Then I packed my luggage, took a bath and added another franc to the little pile. It was later afternoon and I still had several hours before my train. The heat was more intolerable than ever and the air was heavy with coming thunder. For some reason I was very nervous and began pacing the room like a caged animal, sweating profusely and undoing all the good my bath had done me. I stood at the window and watched the forms of lightly dressed women and girls hurrying to and fro under the menacing sky. Peeling off my sweat-drenched shirt I became very lustful, and the summer expired in thunderstorms.

Just a moment ago the train carried me across the Border, and I felt again the strength of the identity which I share with these moors, stones, and men, with this land which made me and whose fate beats in me with heavy insistence. And I knew that this feeling was reality, not sentimentality or illusion. Yet at the same time I thought: this country is defiled with the spirit of judgement. The thought was prompted in me, certainly, by the fact that I have come home to be judged, immediately and in the most literal sense; but it was thrown up from a deeper source too, for has not my whole life, at bottom, been judging, and being judged? I imagine tonight that I have an intuitive insight into the mind of the man who will judge me, that I have an intimate knowledge of the judicial spirit. No doubt I am being most unjust to a worthy individual, perhaps even to the whole race of judges: but for me the image I shall describe is eternal, ineradicable.

In the first place, then, the judicial spirit is the servant not of truth but of society and its needs, and from this perversion arises the complex structure of its hypocritical mechanism, its lying logic. The principles of this structure are in truth prejudices, born of needs and desires, therefore not by reason but only by mental violence can it be met. Yet this fact the judicial spirit has determined never to allow to enter the doors of its consciousness: that its entire being is erected upon false foundations, false because they bear no necessary relation to truth. Its own rules and principles it equates absolutely with truth, and not only will it brook no denial of this equation, it will not even understand how denial should be possible. Yet though it cannot understand its own falsity, unconsciously and deep it *knows* it; imagine, then, the fear and hatred inspired by any who will assert this falsity in its face. That is the source of its domineering attitude, of its claims to an absolute, unanswerable power of command. No judge looks upon any crime with greater abhorrence than upon contempt of court, not even upon rape or murder. Should he let such a challenge pass he flees the defence of his own motive force: his very personality disintegrates before his eyes. I must recognise this imperative if I am to be prepared to meet it.

This then is your character, judge. Because you cannot risk

knowing and questioning yourself, you are eaten up with vanity, with self-love, with an unalterable conviction of your own rightness. The capacity for self-criticism is entirely lacking in you, petrified by your bloated sense of your own worth. Yet paradoxically this lack of self-knowledge does not preclude you from subtlety and shrewdness in your judgment of others, for that after all is your calling. Ignorant of the roots of motivation in your fellow-men, you are nonetheless sure in your analysis of the surface of their character, you are a great mocker and mimic, in a cold, uncharitable spirit. Your own hypocrisy you would angrily deny, for your mind seethes with the prejudices which you unquestioningly take for the truth, and from out of the prejudices springs your mode of reasoning, the endlessly devious and tortuous reasoning of a peasant, a complete system of false logic which true logic cannot reach.

What I hate most about you, judge, is your obtrusive and spurious maleness, the ridiculous splashing of your barrel chest with cold water by which you seek to conceal your hatred of the body, and of the fullness of life, which you detest in others and seek tirelessly to destroy. Closeness and tenderness, all endearments are anathema to you. Because you hate to see other men living you must force your domineering will upon them, enter and control their lives to impoverish and nullify them. So you are brutal, inquisitive, pompous and puritanical. Being entirely society's man you share society's ideals; take it upon yourself, indeed, to be their guardian. Yet because you are uneasily aware of what you lack, how gross is your sentimentality, chest-splasher, when you choose to indulge yourself!

I have long trained myself to hate you, judge, and the time is coming now when I shall face you in open court. What weapons shall I use against you? Those bequeathed to me by my ancestors, whom I love and hate as I love and hate myself. There was a great-great-grandfather of mine, a minister and the harshest of evangelicals, whose sermons I have read; they are written in a style of brutal and naive complexity, their condemnations and threats couched in terms of a chilling formality. I am sure that their author loved God no more than he loved man, but I am sure also that he tried to love God; believing that if one is to live at all one must rely, to some extent, upon counterfeit emotions; not, however, in a spirit of willing self-deception, rather in the hope that if sufficiently persisted in, such emotions might at last become genuine. He sought in God for what he lacked; but what else is lacking can never be found, what is found is something else. His mind, then, I shall use against you: it is one you will understand.

Do not suppose however that my ancestors were all ministers. I have also in my veins the blood of ten generations of butchers, who for two hundred and fifty years slaughtered beasts and chopped up flesh to feed the people of Dalkeith. I do not disbelieve in heredity: when then should I not be a handy man with a cleaver?

The final struggle of our two wills is approaching. I have no knowledge of you, judge, yet I know you. It is the judicial spirit I know: it is the judicial spirit which accuses me, accuses me of not serving it, of not subduing my will to it. It accuses me, and I will answer it, blight for blight.

How much the judicial spirit is my inheritance.

THE SHERIFF-SUBSTITUTE: Is there anything which you wish to say in extenuation of your conduct?

I: I wish to speak in vindication of my conduct. I was not invited to give evidence, I was cited, ordered to do so. Had I been asked in the interests of the truth to deliver myself of the facts as they appeared to me, I would have done so willingly; I would also, had it been considered desirable, have said what I took to be the moral issues involved in the case, and further I would have been willing to justify my views on these issues in free debate with others involved, or invited to participate. All this I would have done as a free man concerned for the truth, not wishing to impose his will upon another, not wishing to pass sentence on another and unwilling to be made use of for such a purpose.

I question both your motives and your methods, sir. You wish me to be your chattel, your possession, you wish to make use of me for ends with which it is possible I will not agree and by means which I would consider intolerable. I do not believe that moral judgment is a matter of training and experience; I believe that I am as capable of judging the moral issues involved in this case as you are, though I do not wish to exercise that capacity; or rather, to extend judgment into condemnation. It has been written that 'The vision of justice is God's pleasure alone'. A man's actions, besides, bring upon him their own deserts in the simplest and most complete of possible manners: they modify what he is. Your punishment for choosing to be a judge, for instance, is that you are a judge and nothing else. Therefore I will not be a party to condemnation.

But I was not ordered here, even, to give the unvarnished facts of the case in my own way. I was ordered here so that my words might be interpreted according to the preconceptions of my questioners. The prosecution would try to make one thing out of my words, the defence something else. The truth might lie somewhere between them, or somewhere else entirely. I might wish to give my opinion of the truth: I might wish to speak only facts. What I could never permit would be for my words to be used in the interests of what I considered falsehood. It is unreasonable to expect any man to be even an unwilling party to a lie. You may tell me that no system could be made to work which I would countenance, that society has to develop practical techniques for establishing standards of justice. I am not concerned with that, I am concerned only with my own moral responsibilities. There will always be plenty of people not only prepared but anxious to do dirty work, and often enough for the worst possible motives.

I will not be used, then, for purposes with which I may dis-
agree—to assist in condemnation—nor to lend countenance to
a judgment with which I may disagree. But beyond that, I will
simply not be used. I am a free man, I am not your possession,
I will co-operate for ends with which I agree, by means with
which I agree, and if I am asked nicely. I will not be coerced.
I demand the right to remain uninvolved if I so wish. If I make
that choice, I remain subject to natural law, and if it is morally
a wrong choice, then I lessen what I am, and that is my pun-
ishment. But I insist that it be my choice, my responsibility. It
is not yours. I do not exist for your benefit or society's. Nor
for my own: I am a free agent before God.

Nor do I believe that your trial of me today is held in the
interests of truth or real justice, it is held in the interests of your
office and your function, in the interests of your own concep-
tion of yourself and your role. I am here because I represent a
threat to you and the system of lies which I have just exposed,
and which passes for justice. You hate freedom and life and
you do not wish anyone else to exercise their capacity for them.
Therefore you lay moral claims to possession of their souls, and
you are prepared to do anything to defend those claims. You
will not believe what I am saying, with any part of you which
you will permit to attain to consciousness. But deeper in you
there is a knowledge that I am right, and which hates me for it.
To that knowledge I address myself: You can do your worst to
me and no doubt will, but you will not possess me or fashion
me to your ends. Your power is of no avail to you, because it
cannot achieve the one end for which you care, the reduction
of my will to the point of subservience to yours.

THE SHERIFF-SUBSTITUTE: I cannot recall that I have
ever had stand accused before me a man of greater pride, of
greater arrogance than you have just shown yourself to be. I
could if I wished amply defend the system of justice which has
been built up by the wisdom and experience of the men of this
country throughout a long history, a system for which you have
expressed unbridled contempt; but it is neither my duty nor my

wish to make apologies for the law. Nor have I anything to say about your virulent attack upon myself in my capacity as the servant of justice and society. In that capacity however you may have no doubts that I will act. I believe that the stand you have taken today was prompted not by the dictates of your conscience but rather by the claims of an assertive will. But whatever your motives, your conduct has been such as strikes at the very roots of justice, and your example, were it to be followed widely, would speedily paralyse the dispensing of justice in the courts of this country. This is a possibility which it is my duty to forestall; it must be made clear to the public that such actions may be expected to incur the severest displeasure of the courts. I prescribe for your pride a period of therapy which I can only hope you will allow to benefit you. I earnestly hope that you will soon come to realise that we are members one of another. I sentence you to a period of three months' imprisonment.

II

At the moment I do not too much mind being in prison; it does not seem so very different from my normal life. I am mercifully alone in this cell—very fortunate in this, I believe—and I have pen and paper. The regimen and conditions of life are not pleasant, it is true, but I have known almost as bad in other places. The one thing which I really miss is being able to walk, a pastime on which I have become very dependent. I can think only under two sets of conditions: with a pen in my hand, and when I am walking. Perhaps also sometimes in the bath; but sitting in an armchair, for instance, or over a meal or a drink, that is hopeless. It is very possible, of course, that before my time is up I will be driven crazy by my physical restriction, but so far I am quite happy. There are two possible interpretations which I can put on this fact. Either my mental freedom is such that my inner being is unaffected by any bonds placed on my body, and my mind can range where it wills in defiance of the limits forced upon me; or else I have lived all my life in shackles, in mental and moral captivity, and physical deprivation is scarcely capable of worsening this state. I favour the former interpretation, of course, but suspect that the latter is the true one.

That day I had the conversation with Alan Bryce he spoke of the violence of my spiritual pride, and now the Sheriff-Substitute has made a similar diagnosis of my condition. One can be right,of course, and at the same time proud. Such a charge requires at least to be gone into. I have been thinking about Hindu doctrines of the self for the last couple of days, and the following comes to mind:

When I was about fifteen I was working one summer after-
noon in the disused stables at school, sawing up some of the
branches which had been scattered all over the ground, and
clearing away the undergrowth and weeks which were clogging
the place. Suddenly I saw something black moving among the
roots of those great thick-stalked weeds which resemble wild
rhubarb (I am no botanist). It turned out to be a black rabbit,
an escaped pet presumably, blinded and horribly deformed and
swollen by myxomatosis, that marvel of modern science. The
rabbit's head was about twice its normal size, the eye sockets
gross and bulbous, and it could hop about only very slowly,
clearly on its last legs. I decided that I would have to kill it,
and looked around for a suitable weapon. Unfortunately all the
branches in the stable were from some tree of very soft wood
(I repeat I am no botanist), with damp mushy bark. There was
nothing else for it but to use one of these branches, however.
A friend of mine had told me once how he had been cycling
down a country road when he had come across about half a
dozen rabbits dying from this disease by the roadside: he had
dismounted and cut the throats of all of them with his penknife.
But such expedients were beyond me. I hoped very much that
I could crack the rabbit's skill with one blow, and it was there-
fore necessary that I should drive it out into the open where I
could get a good aim at it. This rabbit wanted to live, however.
In spite of its horrible condition it was able to sense danger,
and its instinct for self-preservation remained undiminished.
Although it was blind it began to nose further into the thick
tangle of weeks and wild plants, and into the lee of logs and
other obstructions. In great distress I drove it from one place
to another, but never seemed able to get a clear view of it. It
made me shudder to tap its backside with the branch: I thought
of leaving it to die in the course of nature, but I could not bear
to do so. The cruelty of the symptoms of the disease filled me
with nausea, and I was amazed at the animal's stubborn instinctive
determination to live. At last I succeeded in driving it out to
an open space in the middle of the stable, and aimed a strong

blow at its head. I mistimed it, however, or the rabbit hopped on quicker than I expected, and I caught it instead across the back; it fell over on its side. Weeping, I struck it as hard as I could on the skull but it continued to writhe. I dropped the branch and walked round in circles distractedly, shaking from head to foot and close to vomiting. Finally I forced myself to pick up the branch again and I continued to strike the animal's head with the end of the branch until it ceased to squirm.

As with that rabbit, so will it be with my ego, my false self. To kill it is a duty which I ought not to shirk, but a very demanding one: and it is sure to cling stubbornly to its life, to use every means at its disposal to preserve itself. I will try to drive it into the light of day and kill it in open fight, but it will tirelessly seek the neuks and crannies, bury itself in the foliage and reappear as large as life somewhere else. The driving forth of my ego will be an unremitting task, horrible and distasteful but unavoidable. I can kill it or I can die most horribly with it; and once the decision has been taken there will be no going back. Such an undertaking will require all my resources, it will seem at times like self-destruction. Yet it is the only worthy task, at this moment I am convinced of that. I must discover and know its every hiding-place, I must drive it forth, and I must somehow find the strength to go on bludgeoning it until it ceases to squirm.

These notes: my missing offspring—ugly likeness of myself.

Yet what is my self? Where does it begin, where does it? Are the various appearances which I present to others less my self than my own conception of what I am? It is impossible to know how one appears to others, physically even. The mirror image is a static one. For instance, I suspect that I am not graceful in movement, but I do not know. I know that I walk very fast with long strides, that although athletically incompetent I am energetic and can walk great distances; but what I look like in movement I can only surmise. I can give a very accurate description of my mirror image. I am six foot in height and of the long, loose-limbed build, thin but big-boned, and my hands have long bony fingers. Because my chest is shallow and my shoulders are broad, the latter tend to droop, and my head is set forward on my neck. My head is not large, but well-made. In profile it is seen to be of the long narrow type: in full face roughly triangular, tapering from a forehead of average dimensions through good cheekbones to a somewhat receding chin. My brows are good, and my hazel eyes well-set. My nose is my strongest feature, dominating my face in profile. The bone structure is thin, long and markedly arched,but the nose ends a little incongruously in a large, blunt tip. My thick brown hair is cut short, brushed forward and unparted. The mouth is small and well-formed. My complexion is of the most girlish pink and white and flushes readily. This tendency to femininity is countered however by my prominent nose and by some indefinable quality in the whole. I can tell that I have a good enough speaking voice, unexpectedly deeply pitched, but I speak with no claims to natural ease or fluency, in an unobtrusive Edinburgh accent.

But when I have said all this I have said practically nothing about even my physical appearance. It is only the mirror image. I do not know what I look like laughing or eating, or sitting reading in an armchair, or in an animated conversation, or embarrassed, or angry. I do not know what my face looks like when it takes on that sullen set which has been criticised by some people, or when I am drunk. I do not know the inflections of my voice and what they reveal. The body in fact is nothing except when it is in action, and when it is in action we are too absorbed to notice it. The mirror image therefore, like the photograph, in presenting us with a static instead of a dynamic picture of ourselves acts as a distorting influence upon the sensibility. It involves a pose, a stylisation answering to certain needs or preconceptions. Similarly I perceive now, reading over these notes, that they are the mirror image of my soul. They present a picture of my soul seen through the lenses of certain attitudes and predeterminations. The special limitation here is not that of being unable to witness action, but of having to pick and choose, and to do so inevitably for some ulterior motive which may involve, not a gross distortion, but an essentially new creation, new because it is independent of the other influences and considerations which in reality share in the nature of the whole. A man with a raging toothache, for instance, is totally concerned with his toothache and not at all with the blooming health of the remaining nine hundred and ninety-nine thousandths of his body. Thus though I have written only about myself and no word which I did not mean, I can scarcely recognise myself in this journal. For the soul also is real only in action, and not in the mirror image. If I have difficulty in recognising myself in these passages, would there be any chance at all of my old landlady Mrs Keith recognising the polite, charming, fresh-faced, considerate young laddie who was her best-ever tenant? Yet again, was that young laddie ever really me?

Yet one has to start somewhere, and by a curious process the reality becomes increasingly more like the mirror image. Alan Bryce said that I was proud, the Sheriff-Substitute said that I was proud and arrogant, and I am forced to admit that any reader of this journal would be likely to say much the same thing, to interpret in this way the mirror image I have made myself; whereas I have always thought of myself rather as a rigorous but valiant soldier for truth. To myself I have seemed not proud, but right. So it seems that the time has come for a re-examination, an investigation of roots. Is my arrogance destroying me? Has my wilfulness been always in pursuit of the truth.

An incident last winter, for instance. It must have been about February, for it was several weeks since I have been able to get out for a proper country walk. One day I became very bored by the city and irritated by the continuance of the bad weather which was thwarting me in this way. There was snow on the hills and filthy slush on the pavements. Some small schoolgirls came splashing past me, singing coarsely and piercingly,

My bonnie lies over the ocean,
My bonnie lies over the sea,
My father lies over my mother,
And that is why I am here.

They showered slush over my shoes and trouser-legs; I walked on furiously, drawn together in thin disgust. I made up my mind without further hesitation that in spite of the total unsuitability of the conditions I would go for a walk in the hills and breathe the unsullied air in my own company. I got the car and drove up to Threipmuir: by the time I arrived I was singing happily.

When I began to walk, however, my coat collar pulled up above my ears, along the familiar path beside the reservoir which in good weather made exhilarating, hospitable walking, my happiness soon turned to demoniac rage. I found it impossible to keep my footing in a morass of frozen snow, puddles and mud, and a piercing buffeting wind off the snow-covered hills was blowing full into my face. The only sensible and reasonable thing would have been to have turned back at once and gone instead for a relaxing little run in the car. But I had come up here for a walk, and a walk I was going to have. I began cursing my rubber soles aloud, swearing at my slow progress, shouting defiance at the elements. Then I felt my teeth setting together and my eyes popping out of their sockets, and I was crashing my heels down into the frozen snow, my legs completely rigid and unbending, every muscle in my thighs and stomach flexed against the conditions underfoot, my completely numbed face thrusting forward into the teeth of the wind. I must have looked like a raving lunatic. I had set my running eyes upon a post at the end of the straight, about half a mile away, and I could reach it or perish. Thus I lurched and slipped on, my heels crashing and thudding into the ice and puddles. Every time I slipped or stumbled, I charged on with renewed vigour, faster than ever, and I could hear animal noises of exhilaration escaping from my throat. Before long I realised that I was shouting at the top of my voice: 'God strike me down if I don't reach that post! God strike me down! Damn you, wind, you'll not stop me! I'll not be stopped by any elements!' I was shrieking these phrases through my teeth until my throat ached: my heart seemed lunging up through the roof of my mouth. Then I became terrified that God was indeed going to strike me down, that I was simply going to burst my heart. Yet I could not stop, on the contrary I redoubled my exertions at this thought. I had ceased to make intelligible sounds but a protracted shriek was issuing somehow from my lungs, which was scarcely distinguishable from the sound of the wind. I staggered on, rigid, clawing with my hands at the elements that were assaulting me, on and on and on I lurched, and at last my hands were upon the woodenpost and I sand to my knees, semi-conscious, but laughing. I had done what I had set out to do and God had not struck me down.

But on the slow journey back to the car I was for the first time in my life truly concerned for my sanity; and with the wind at my back I felt humbled and puny, and lonely and sick unto death.

It is a long-standing tradition among intellectual prisoners to kill some of their wearier hours by reading the Bible. Traditionally, it is the only book to which they can gain access, and this happy state of affairs leads inevitably to a revolution in their spiritual lives. I am fortunate in having access to several other books and at first I saw no reason why I should perpetuate the cliché. Yesterday, however, when I was thinking how glad I was that I had no need to do so, it occurred to me that this was perhaps a therapy which I had a duty to undertake, as part of my programme for chastening my ego. For I have for some years been exceedingly frightened of the Bible; and my failure to reread it seems to me now an inexcusable self-indulgence, a form almost of stupidity, as I understand the term. Stupidity: how pervasive is that most subtle of moral vices, from which only an exceptionally strong soul can hope to be entireley free. It must be in earliest childhood that the soul learns to be stupid, learns to protect itself from the truth by refusing to understand—and once that way has been chosen, how useless, how inconceivable, to think of going back! The mind, naturally open, becomes on all sides closed, no ray of truth is allowed to force its way through its dulled windows, physically almost it hardens and crustifies. And related to this is the refuge of jargon, of language violated, wherein words become sacrosanct, holy in all their inadequacy and inaccuracy, used as a barrier against the truth by virtue of their concealments and their failings, above all by their capacity to engender a false, plausible world of their own, which the credulous can be persuaded to accept as corresponding to the real world.

I decided to begin my therapy gently, by reading the book of Jonah, which as first seemed to me to have lost its disturbing edge as a result of the comfortable proverbiality which it has attained. But before long I began to doubt if this was really so. The puzzling quality of the story came back to me: I had always found it difficult to relate together the two parts of the allegory, and yet it was just in the elusiveness of the connection that the disturbing nature of the book lay. So I would make a determined effort to understand Jonah; and I reached certain tentative conclusions.

Jonah, then, was an honest man, one naturally predisposed in favour of the truth; the word of the Lord came directly to him. But Jonah seeing the wickedness of Nineveh, could not for once bring himself to contemplate that truth nor its consequences: for he had not come to terms with his God. It is not that he feared the sinners of Nineveh; rather he feared its falling towers, and he feared the unsubdued pride within his own soul. And so, though seeing the truth, he sought to abdicate from the situation which filled him with dread, and he resolutely turned his face away from Nineveh, in whose fate he reluctantly found himself involved. A profound terror had taken root within him, and it was this form which he sought to escape; its palpable occasion lying for him in the wrath of the Lord towards Nineveh. And this is what was peculiar about Jonah: that in his heart he understood his condition very well.

So he took ship for Tarshish; for Tarshish where he hoped to be removed from the context in which he would be required to regulate his will: for the latter ends of the earth. Yet when the storm overtook him, Jonah was not surprised; rather, it gave him pleasure to observe the inescapable pattern of the fate which God had prepared for him to bring his will to reluctant submission. He felt that he must play out the game to a conclusion that was inevitable: he must not intervene in the pattern of truth. Therefore, instead of humbling his will, he desired the sailors to still the storm by throwing him to the waves. For it was hard, too hard for him to make himself nought in unequivocal contemplation of the truth. He must make it necessary for God to send him first into the abyss: he must test wisdom by the scale of folly and of madness.

Now Jonah was no ordinary soul and his pride was no ordinary conceit. So it was that in the hell of the fish's belly Jonah found his truth; even in that hopelessness, that watery nullity,he perceived the perfection of God's will. In that very zero Jonah was able to see and anticipate grace. For there was no further journey now that he could make along the path of pride, avid as he was for the soul's ultimates. In the fish's belly he encountered an absolute; in turning his face towards God's holy temple he experienced a mercy which had always existed and would always exist; its power of visible action being but a temporal form. Hell to Jonah became grace in his repentance because even there he could turn his face towards God. So that when the fish vomited out Jonah upon the dry land, he emerged perfect in truth; now indeed must he arise and cry against Nineveh.

Does it not seem to rankle, that here the story of Jonah does not end? Is the action not perfect and complete? Had not Jonah become united to the truth of God?

To the truth of God, yes, but not to his love.

For Jonah, no longer at odds with himself, and with his dread behind him, now longed mercilessly to witness the destruction of Nineveh, filled as he was with understanding of the wickedness of that great city. He despised the stupidity of the city's inhabitants, who sinned because they were unable to discern between their right hand and their left hand. And what he despised he also hated. As for him, he stood inact in his own rightness; he had forbidden himself to intervene in the fate of his own soul, and he desired for Nineveh a similar purity of fate, a just chastisement and retribution. Only the people of Nineveh had souls less strong than his, and their sins could be purged, he thought, only in destruction. It was only for the sake of the truth of justice that he was compelled to give them warning.

But something happened the possibility of which had never occurred to Jonah: the people of Nineveh took heed of his warning, they turned from their evil ways and repented. And God pardoned and spared them. Then Jonah was doubly angry and mortally angry. He was angry not only because he had been robbed of the prospect of a cruel justice and because what he had foretold had not occurred; more profoundly, he was angry with God and jealous of him because he perceived a mercy and a love which he himself lacked and of which he was incapable. And God himself, even, was unable to make real to Jonah by way of illustration the nature of his love and mercy: since Jonah was able to show pity for the gourd only because he was himself its beneficiary, whereas God's sparing of Nineveh was the fruit of love alone. For Jonah's mode was the mode of truth and not of love: and it is possible that it is not given to one soul to be perfect both in truth and in love.

In the fish's belly Jonah united himself to the will of the God of truth, and there his repentance was perfect; but the God of love remained unborn within his heart. We know that God spared Nineveh, if only for a time: but of Jonah we do not hear the fate. Was Jonah only of import, then, in that his warning changed the hearts of the people of Nineveh? Was this the true value of his resurrection from the fish's belly? Or, on the contrary, did Nineveh and all its thousands and its much cattle only serve as a touchstone by means of which could be tested and developed the relationship of Jonah to his God? Or were the fate of Jonah and the fate of Nineveh not separable at all, but only different aspects of an indivisible movement of divine will? I do not know. But of this much I'm sure: that Jonah found grace at the direst moment, at the extreme low point of his spiritual sojourn, by the act of perceiving it there. And that is perhaps some ground for hope.

Falsehood can be absolute as truth.

Few of us are totally strangers to lies, the lies of others and of ourselves, the lies of conceit, convenience and self-deceit which render life more bearable, more comfortable, more flattering and more vile; these receive acceptance and are even made venial by virtue of their primitive order, of our knowledge that they are perpetrated for comprehensible purposes and serve understandable needs, however base; for on such knowledge rests our confidence that limits are set to their sway. But I knew, once, a man whose lying finally terrified me; and not so much for the monstrosity of its extent as for what seemed the anarchy of its rule.

He was an employee of a firm for which I once worked on a holiday job as a temporary clerk, a lugubrious family business in Leith nostalgic for the commercial grandeurs of the nineteenth century but making grudging attempts to adapt itself to the business world of 1960. I first ran across Tom Bremner, which was the name by which he went but which I can no longer have grounds for confidence in supposing his real one, in the staff canteen, where his conversation, consisting mainly of scathing condemnations of the idiocies of office procedure and satirical sallies against other members of the staff, had however this sole but priceless merit, that it was unconcerned with football. For this reason alone I came to welcome his company over lunch, and sometimes during the lunch hour I would take a stroll with him in the docks. He was a smallish man in his middle twenties with thinning hair and horn-rimmed glasses, always neatly dressed and of punctiliously refined accent, harmless looking yet at the same time unwholesome somehow, I felt—even before I caught him out in the first of an infinitely extending series of lies; one which was to prove typical in its utter pointlessness and unaccountability. I had asked him casually in what department he worked, and he had told me the wholesale department; yet a day or two later I discovered that he in fact worked and had always worked in the customs room, and had at no stage had any connection with the wholesale department. At the time I shrugged this off as some kind of misunderstanding, but soon I became aware of frequent discrepancies and anomalies of the same sort occurring in even the most casual information imparted by him.

Our acquaintanceship never became intimate, but over the weeks the range of our conversation naturally extended itself, and I was led to consider whether one possible source of his deceit might be sought in his indefatigable snobbery. He was at constant pains to impress upon me his high social standing, was given to an odious habit of name-dropping and to providing dreary accounts of the doings of his supposed relatives, such as 'my uncle, you know the one that's a director in the herring industry—mind you of course he never comes into contact with the actual herrings.' To the account of this snobbery might be laid a whole series of misrepresentations, such as that during his National Service he had been a Lieutenant in the Royal Scots, when I was later to discover incontrovertible evidence that he had in reality been a Lance-Corporal in the Pay Corps. He might reasonably have hoped to get away with that one, but it was rather too much to expect even so apparently naive a youth as myself to swallow the metamorphosis, in the space of a fortnight, of Tom Bremner's father from managing director of a Princes Street store to Vice-Chairman of the South of Scotland Electricity Board. This instance exemplifies two aspects of the anarchy of his fictionalising: that he did not scruple to make statements which could with the greatest ease be refuted by a little easy checking, and that he had apparently no consciousness of contradicting himself, which he did frequently, lavishly, and sometimes after a space of as little as a couple of days. For a time, indeed, I began to suspect that he was trying to make a fool of me, so clumsy and obvious were his lies, that his object was to test how gross a lie he would have to tell me before I would protest; for in most ways he didn't appear stupid. But my enquiries among other members of the staff assured me that he was indeed notorious as a liar, to the extent that his company had become to many an embarrassment to be shunned.

Nor was his snobbery alone sufficient to account for his predilection for falsehoods. There were many, indeed, from which no conceivable advantage could accrue to him, by way of others' estimation of him or in any other terms. Why should he tell me that his father's name was Thoms, like his own, when the telephone directory listed him as Peter. R. Bremner? Why should he announce that he had acquired a new Ford Popular, and drive up the next morning in a new car indeed, but a Morris Minor? I began to discover a certain fascination in such questions. I started, at first in an effort to counteract what would otherwise have been the unremitting boredom of his company, to take a note of what he said, check whatever could be verified or refuted, and then list his many deceptions and contradictions, in order to seek in them some pattern, some controlling purpose, even some psychological coherence. But I was quite unable to find any. And it was at this point that I began to be in a strange way frightened by this inexplicable phenomenon. For one thing, any normal sense of stability disappeared in conversation with him; it was disconcerting to be quite unable, even when trivial subjects were under discussion, to rely on the truth of anything he said. A lie told for a purpose, however degrading, can be placed and accounted for, but Bremner's anarchic lies seemed an offence against the principles of order itself. So the more I began to suspect that they had no cause, the more necessary it became to find one; and the only way to do so appeared to be to confront him with his lies. Yet it was already too late for this, and the longer I left it the more impossibly embarrassing such a move would become. I could not at all, moreover, envisage its consequences; but somehow I seemed to sense that they would be devastating. I felt thoroughly uneasy.

As it was, I did nothing; after three months I left the job, and shortly afterwards I went away from the city. Later, home on holidays, I ran across Tom Bremner a few times, and once or twice even had a pint with him. He was growing seedier and his hair was becoming more moth-eaten; he had changed his job several times and seemed to be drifting without direction; but he was still dropping names and telling lies. I remember thinking that I could imagine no future for him, that it was impossible to conceive of his life stretching indefinitely on into the future on this vein. So it was with a certain shock indeed, but also with a sense of its fitness, that I read in the papers one day some three years after I had last seen him, that Tom Bremner had gassed himself in his Marchmont flat on a New Year's morning.

It had scarcely occurred to me that before his otiose life was capable, perhaps compounded, of suffering; but in retrospect I now saw each one of his futile lies as an element of a labyrinthine pattern to which I had been denied access, a dazzling structure which he had raised between himself and darkness, which had assumed its own infinitely complex logic and twisted desperately from his control, towards an ever thinner and more precarious fragility. Until someone, bored at last with this unaccountable maze, had torn it rudely apart, as only cowardice had stayed me from tearing it, and revealed to the eyes of Tom Bremner in a sudden rush the black chaos from which it had protected him: and this chaos had gulped him down whole. But this surmise of mine is perhaps only a piece of romanticising; in the last analysis I know nothing of his case.

From the onset I must have believed stubbornly in the unity of the spiritual and physical worlds. And I do not doubt that in this respect I have at times been somewhat lacking in humour. When I was about ten years old, for instance, I was invited to a children's fancy-dress ball, and determined that I would go in the guise of Mozart. For weeks I studied pictures of the master in various books that I had discovered, and in choosing my clothes at the hire-shop I kept these images clearly in my mind. The day arrived: I took infinte pains over my toilet and dress, particularly the wig and hose, took a last look at my pictures and judged myself a fairish replica. The ball passed without incident and no more tediously than I had expected; no special remark had been passed on my costume, but this was quite to my taste. Towards the end, however, a woman whom my mother knew came up to me beamingly and said, 'Oh, I do like your costume, it's lovely! But isn't it a pity there are so many eighteenth century gentlemen?' I was both astonished and offended; and in my chilliest tone I replied, 'But there is only one Mozart.' Yet on further enquiry I was forced to the unwelcome conclusion that nobody but myself was aware that I was Mozart.

Why were the two worlds not one? Confronted with this unspoken question I began slowly to sense that my stubbornness on this score represented a striving to repair a rift in the natural driving force within me. And to understand this I must turn now to my beloved forebears, to those Old Testament men whose denials have not ceased to block the upsurge of my being. Supported by a new-found and cruel faith and revelling in the freedom of their own consciences they arose from the happy obscurity of the ancestral life which they denied, to acquire for themselves wealth and power. Their self-assertion they learned amply to justify with reasons and to sanctify with faith. And from this theological source grew ultimately the virulent logical systems and merciless disputes in which my mind was trained and sharpened, which flayed it and left it raw.

They began to stir about three centuries ago, those ancestors of mine, awakened by religious ferment, tentatively they began to emerge, rubbing their eyes, from among the Lammermuir foothills where they had tilled the soil or tended their flocks perhaps since the days of the Votadini. At first they moved cannily, shifting their ground and not much more; one of them became a servant and then a tenant of the Fletchers at Saltoun. Doubtless he was an example of that new phenomenon, the God-fearing man, with a weather eye open for his own advancement or that of his children. It was shortly after this that bleaching was introduced to Scotland, and by a stroke of fortune it made its first appearance at Saltoun, Lady Fletcher having smuggled the secret out of Holland in a walking-stick. A Straiton was on the scene, and he prospered, breaking out with this new trade in all directions. He and his sons leased bleachfields at Saltoun, Glencorse, Kinchie, Ednam and Ford. In due course he became an elder of the parish, served it with devotion, died and was honourably buried; but his well-earned rest was soon interrupted, for his body was lifted from its grave by body-snatchers, to be sold for dissection by the anatomists. He was one of the first fruits and victims of the age of money.

Among his children, and there were many of them, an uneasy restlessness began to show itself. They must all have wanted to advance their fortunes, and some of them failed, they sank back into obscurity or emigrated to try again. There were so many of them that there was never enough money to go round, but they had grown hard and resourceful. One of them, a bleacher, seeing that bleaching was about to decay, decided to become a miller and a brewer as well, and was able to bring up seven children in fair prosperity. The brother of this miller, a lad o'pairts evidently, had distinguished himself in medicine and then in the Church and in addition had married a lady of fortune. Having

57

no heirs he became the patron of his many nephews, shipping the illegitimate ones off to Canada and setting up the favoured in well-stocked farms at home. Some of them moved away and some finally failed and went bankrupt, their children scattering to America, to New Zealand, or China, to make good or to die young—as one did from a bullet in the back in a Western tavern. The youngest of the nephews, however, an exceedingly pious man, made a success of farming and eventually established his pre-eminent status in the neighbourhood. This was my great-grandfather. He married the daughter of the United Presbyterian minister of the parish, a participant in the Disruption of the Church in 1843 and a man undoubtedly of strong evangelical views. Thirteen children were born of this match, of whom not all lived up to the piety of their background. One indeed is said to have been a drunkard, for whose soul his father could be heard praying nightly in terrifying wails and moans, his spade beard jutting upwards to heaven. But the more provident and responsible members of the brood scattered once more to seek their fortunes, and this generation it was that turned their faces finally towards the city, for the countryside which had raised them no longer offered their ambitions sufficient scope, or answered to their inner needs. The youngest of them all was my grandfather; he left Dalkeith High School and set out for Edinburgh with little money in his pocket to become an apprentice in the grain trade in the port of Leith. Being industrious and very shrewd he rose in the firm and was taken into partnership, and after some time was able to buy his partner out, and establish himself as a prosperous merchant. So the Straitons had fastened their grip upon life and did not mean to let go; and it must have seemed as if their ultimate destiny had been achieved.

Of all the branches of my ancestry, all the spokes of the wheel of which I am the hub, the story has been very similar. The primacy of faith, the emptiness of works, freed their wills for the drive towards material ends, the gradual abandonment and rejection of their past, the inexorable march towards wealth and influence, towards the inescapable ethos of the city. Rebels there must have been, a few in whom the natural impulse towards free life was not immediately diverted, in whom it sought for a way up and out. There is one collateral forebear in particular about whom I often think, who, I believe, was ultimately broken by the extremities of his desires. The family used to call him the Fiery Star. I cannot with any authority claim to enter his mind for I know only the bare facts of his life. Perhaps he was really nothing but a lazy wastrel and drunkard, but I like to think that he could have been more. As a young man he started milling under his father, but this he soon abandoned to join the army. Authority in any form seems to have been little to his taste, for he deserted twice; on one occasion the mill was searched for him while he was hiding there, but he was not found. His brothers, who wanted him out of the way, then shipped him to Australia, but before long he managed to stow away to return home on a ship called the 'Fiery Star'. He was one of twenty stowaways found on board after the ship had sailed. In the Indian Ocean one night she caught fire, and the crew and passengers took to the boats, abandoning the stowaways on board. The blaze was sighted by a passing ship, however, and the stowaways were almost miraculously rescued; and as George Straiton was lifted clear of the burning wreck, it is related, in a state of semi-consciousness, he said quite clearly, 'The life-boats have gone down and all are lost.' And indeed no trace of them was ever seen again. After this he was sent to America in the early 1870's but again contrived to get home, and was immediately shipped out again. After some years he returned home and was boarded out in Orkney where he lay low until the general pardon of deserters at the Queen's jubilee in 1887. After that he frequently came from Orkney to Edinburgh, all expenses being charged to his brothers at the mills, who had to support him all his life, presumably as the price for his keeping out of the way. It is said that the first intimation that he had arrived was invariably a bill for a wreath for his mother's grave; eventually he would make his appearance in a cab. When he needed money for drink in Orkney he would do a day's work as a baker. He died there in 1905, unmarried, and there he is buried. It seems a sad ending to an adventurous tale. He may of course have been happy, who knows, but I cannot help suspecting that his desire for an individual life of his own, though he achieved that, brought him nothing else but loneliness, misery and failure. It is good at least to know that he made the Straitons pay for it, in the most literal way, and the only one they would have understood. I imagine him as one of their most distressful victims.

Anything I might conclude about the Fiery Star, nevertheless, would be only conjecture. When I consider it, the truth is that I feel only a very superficial identity with him, and attraction towards him. He was an attractive rebel, a colourful figure, but finally fruitless, a dead end. My deeper feelings are for the real Straitons among my forebears. It is them I know: their flesh and minds and spirit are mine, they gave them to me. I love and hate them as I love and hate myself; and I love and hate myself greatly. I have walked in the places where they walked, and sat down in the churches where they worshipped, and have felt that they acknowledged me, and that I understood their lives. I have stood beside their graves in a remote churchyard in late autumn, and my flesh has crept up to the grand words to which their souls thrilled, and which set their faces like rock: 'I know that my Redeemer liveth, and that he shall stand at the latter day upon the earth. And though after my skin worms destroy this body, yet in my flesh shall I see God.' Somehow they turned their very affirmations into denials, and that tendency of the will above all is what they have bequeathed to me, their heir. I seem very different from them, but I am not. My concerns and desires are alien from theirs, the disease of the will is the same. I have striven to assert my true life, but I have done so in the *spirit* of denial, that is the whole truth, as I suddenly see it. And here I have brought myself, or my ancestors have brought me, it is all the same. It is they who have built these four prison walls within which I now find myself confined. And equally it is I who have built them around myself: for I remain inescapably one of them.

The walls of this cell are pressing upon my body, constricting it to the point of suffocation: as in one of my recurrent nightmares, in which I am crawling further and further into a narrow tunnel until I am wedged so fast that I can move neither forwards nor backwards. Is this what it is like, I wonder, in the belly of a whale? Alan Bryce told me once, when we were looking at the whale skeleton in the museum, that there was a recorded case of a man being swallowed by a whale and after a considerable time coming out alive. This, I presume, to prove, by implication, that the Jonah story could have been literally true. As if I cared! What does it matter whether it happened or not? But the interesting point was that this man came out, Alan said, as white as the driven snow—the action of some chemical in the animal's guts or mouth. A symbol of the truth Jonah found in the fish's belly. But subsequently the man died.

Jonah emerged perfect in truth, I said earlier—did I hope for a similar purification for myself as a result of my imprisonment? Well, the nearest approach to such cleansing to which I can so far lay claim is a grisly insight into the manner in which I have served the truth: for I am ready now to believe the fable of the man who insisted that the earth was flat. My assertion has been a little more subtle, but really of the same nature: he scorned the objective truth, but my boast has been that it alone has been my god. But I have worshipped it not because I loved it, but because it provided an excellent testing-ground for the exercise of my will. Now at last I have said it. And if I could thus make use of my god, could I not also betray it? No, I will not pursue this thought any further.

It has always been an odd superstitious facet of my mind, and one that I have not succeeded in shaking off, that before I can assimilate any thought and rely upon it, it is necessary for me to speak it aloud; just as before I came here I had constantly to assure myself of the validity and reality of my life by regularly reviewing and reordering the relics I carried around with me wherever I went: photographs, certificates, diaries, notebooks. The converse is that when I have voiced any thought, even if I have not properly weighed and considered it, it becomes for me an inviolable part of my make-up. So it was that this morning I came to realise that I have reached the point of no return: simply, and somewhat to my own surprise, by saying as much aloud. And now I am committed to that fact, it will compel my actions in the direction it demands. For over a month I have written nothing in this journal, for I have been struggling for breath in a mental atmosphere so thin, subtle and rarified, so lacking in substance, that it has not even admitted of any reduction to concept. Now that must end if I am not to lose my reason, so much has become obvious to me. I have reached the point where I am in the most imminent danger of losing the whole motive structure of my life, my belief in truth and in the efficacy of my own will. Now it is true that I started out at the beginning of my imprisonment with the intention of producing just such an effect, and that to lose one's life may very well be to find it. But I can sense that somewhere I have taken the wrong path, that I have been going about things out of a wrong state of mind and in an unhealthy spirit. Nothing, at any rate, will be gained if I end up by losing my mind. My efforts to destroy my ego have been extraordinarily unfruitful, uncoordinated and lacking in direction. I am choking and suffocating in evil.

I have heard that it is a not uncommon thing to dream that the secret of the universe, though remaining elusive, is all but within one's grasp. This experience has not been mine; instead, I have frequently dreamt, and just recently very often, that I am within an ace of understanding the nature of a foul and ultimate evil which is about to envelope me. This evil, which presents itself only as a thick, cloying weight pressing heavily on the doors of my consciousness, is analogous to nothing which the waking mind could comprehend, to no human barbarity or natural calamity, to no recognisable mental torment or horrible imagining. It is more final, complete and comprehensive, and also of a different order. Its terror lies in the fact that it has no form, though the sleeping mind struggles vainly to endow it with one. It is for all men yet at the same time it is for me alone, and it will come about through my most grievous fault. It makes its appearance suddenly, in the middle of an ordinary dream of no great meaning: I feel a strange warning sensation, then with a shock I instantly recognise its presence, it imbues all the insignificant happenings of the dream with its sickly quality of doom. Eventually I wake up in a state of profound shock and lie half dazed, trying to persuade myself that it is only the sum of many unconscious fears and trepidations trying to find themselves a tangible form; but it remains the most disturbing experience which I have known, a genuine *haunting*. And the frequency with which it has oppressed my nights since my imprisonment seems to me an indication that I am going a bit off the rails; in plain blunt terms.

It is just as well that in a week I shall be out of here: for alone in this cell it is beyond me to counteract this desperate plunge into introspection. The struggle I have been going through has utterly worn me out, has all but broken my will and reduced me to nothing. Of course I asked for all this, I willed that it should happen, indeed planned it in a sense, I have neglected to plant the seeds of any better life within me; if I destroy me 'raison d'être' I am left with nothing. I am desperately in need of rest: and in the interests of self-preservation, I shall have to lead a careful, neutral, passionless life for a time—and among strangers. For while I need the presence of people now, at such a time as this my enemies would be all too quick to spot my weakness, fall upon me and devour me. What I need now is a simple, callous detached life among the things of the flesh, for which I long. Then perhaps I can slowly let a new starting-point emerge from the hard soil of my life. I would like to make a museum collection of my past; to have all its aspects arrayed neatly before my eyes, museum items which I cannot touch and which cannot touch me, unalterable and out of use, so that I can rely on their completedness and so dismiss them. Then they will be something solid and external to my new life, compartmentalised by my mind. Assuredly this is a very corrupt need but I am very tempted to satisfy it, because my repose seems to depend upon its satisfaction. The present and the past, now and then, separate: my dearest hope was to be a man of the dawn, but I know that irrevocably I am a man of the sunset.

III

When I was released from prison it was mid-winter, and I was bleakly glad to see the natural order reflecting, as it seemed, the hollowness of death within me. The first two months of the year are the time when I habitually suffer the profoundest metaphysical disorder; but this year no such terrors were capable of disturbing me, for during the course of my time in prison and my inner explorations there, the feeling and experiencing faculties of my mind had spent themselves and atrophied to an exceptional degree. Instead, a formless desolation swathed me about. My spiritual exhaustion was like that of the body when it has emerged from a lonely and racking fever; when the ache and inflammation have departed from the limbs but left them tender, weak and fragile. It was about the festive season when I regained my freedom, but I would see no one; I immured myself in my small flat and lay almost wholly blank for days at a time. When I went out for a walk it was to areas where I knew I would meet nobody of my acquaintance, around Canonmills or down to Leith, where I would wander for hours around the docks, scarcely aware of my surroundings and with only the most meagre thoughts in my head. Although I could not have faced human communication, I felt nonetheless oddly undisturbed and free from worry; for the first time in my life, perhaps, I was taking things just as they came, feeling it impossible to be deeply affected by anything. I remembered how once, when I was waiting in I don't know what station for a train to take me I can't remember where, I had got talking with a worn, dead-faced man of late middle age who had warned me against the ideals of youth. He had long since ceased to believe in anything at all, he said, and since that time he had found an unalterable contentment. I had been sickened them by the inviting stench of his disintegration; I understood his condition intellectually, but not immediately. Now I understood it immediately: I imagined myself a finished man, perceived in that memory a frightful image of what I might become. But even this thought was detached from any emotion and did almost nothing to stir my apathy. I saw the New Year in quite alone, with a couple of bottles of beer, the fire on and the lights out, listening bemused to the sounds of companionable revelry which again and again approached and receded beneath my window: shouting and singing voices, buckets and cans being kicked, cars revving up, cold weather and warm spirits. I did not even bother to look out of the window.

In this condition, without enthusiasm, I determined first of all to be on the move again. I took a train south; that is, in the most hopeless direction. I passed through London; untouched and unmoved I passed through its palpable evil. Nothing had power to touch me. I was seeking nothing and that was what I found. I then took another train—west this time, for I had a vague desire to see Cornwall. I went as far as I could go in that direction. In Penzance one night I had a girl in my hotel bedroom, but the experience did little to help me and I resumed masturbating. Struggle, struggle, struggle, energy amid pessimism. Soon I returned home, determined to be done with travel. Travel solves nothing, being only an anodyne for the pains of the questioning will: in the long run it merely disturbs me always. For instance, a year or two back I made a trip by ocean liner. It is true that there are disadvantages at least of equal gravity attendant upon all other modes of travel, but for the disruption of equilibrium, none can rival the ocean liner. When you first step from the gangplank into the ship you are not surprised to be somewhat confused, and it may be that you are guided to your cabin without being much intimidated by the mazes of stairs, passages and corridors through which you pass; if, indeed, your memory and sense of direction are good, you may without great difficulty regain your point of departure. But when you attempt to apprehend the symmetry of the vessel, you are at once made aware of many grounds for disturbance.

There is no centre of gravity on an ocean liner, for focal points proliferate upon every level: but the location of such a point upon any one deck in unpredictable, there are no grounds for determining from which of the many stairs and companionways it should be approached. Moreover the various classes merge into one another in an indeterminate way—often it is impossible to say where one class ends and another begins, and on each deck the dividing-line, if apprehensible, is at a different point. Some public rooms and some facilities, besides are common to more than one class, while others are strictly segregated. Some signs and notices are clear, other ambiguous, while a few seem to be inviting you to ignore or disobey them. It is useless to try to systematise such a structure in your mind; using different stairs, for instance, you will reach different conclusions even as to the number of decks on the ship.

Nor is any clearer conception obtained by a move to the outer decks. As you go up deck by deck you will be uncertain by which stairs it is best to ascend. By using some you will miss out a deck, arriving two above or even below that from which you started, and similar difficulties attend your horizontal progress. Rounding a corner you will find your way barred, making it impossible for you to complete a circuit, by a sudden change of level, or a CREW ONLY notice, or a division between classes. Corridors and covered walks are without warning blocked or truncated, and as you retrace your steps you forget precisely what aspects of the ship's construction you were attempting to ascertain, your attention being constantly diverted by casual enigmas. From the vantage-point of the rails the relationship between the open deck below you and the interiors through which you have walked appears impenetrably obscure.

As the ship steams out of the dock and begins to turn, its relation to the buildings on the shore alters and you begin to confuse port with starboard and even bow with stern. As you move out to sea all landmarks appear to be slightly in the wrong place and in the wrong relation to each other, and this is confirmed by a consultation with maps and charts. Islands particularly are out of alignment and their identification becomes a matter of doubt.

Once the land has been left behind you become slowly reconciled to the vessel's lack of symmetry, and accept that its construction contains certain anomalies whose purpose you will never penetrate. Fresh sources of disequilibrium are then ready to assail you. There are, first, the constant readjustments demanded of your sense of balance as the state of the sea alters; so that even in calm weather you remain at all times slightly on guard, while in rough you must accustom yourself to the deck's alternately forcing itself upon you and deserting you, must train yourself to anticipate its monotonous ficklenesses. Then as you travel from east to west or from west to east you are endlessly losing or gaining time: the security of the twenty-four hour clock is left behind you on dry land. Either your sleep is brutally curtailed night after night, or the evening extends itself in an endless dreary waste; and sometimes, when they subtract half an hour from the middle of the day, your breakfast and lunch justle one another in sickening proximity. Moreover if you have an inside cabin with no access to the natural light, the sense of time, as you lie in your bunk, disappears altogether, and waking up, you are uncertain whether you have slept for an hour or missed your breakfast. It does without saying that indoors or out you are always either too hot or too cold; distastefull smells, too, stale and rotten as water in which flowers have been left for too long, waft up and down the corridors and smite the nostrils suddenly as you turn a corner. And if you fall into a doze in a deck-chair ther is constantly a dead weight pressing, like conscience, on a certain point on the top of your skull.

Nothing aboard an ocean liner has any substantiality: from the outset you are demoralised, and thought everything presses upon you and importunes you, none of it confers any sense of permanence or solidity. It is one of the affections of an ocean liner to be a microcosm of society, and to persuade you of this there are drapers', tobacconists' and barbers' shops, cinemas, swimming-pools, gambling saloons, bars, dance floors, libraries, hospitals with doctors and nurses, crêches, church services, banks, ping-pong, photographers, laundries and news-sheets, all of them competing for your custom or attention; the ears are continuously assaulted by news broadcasts, recordings of light or classical music, statements from the Captain about progress, position and weather prospects, and blasts on the ship's whistle; there are entertainments which combine the vulgarity of a holiday camp with that of Grand Hotel. Above all there are the horrors of social intercourse with people whom you neither know nor wish to know, who sit with you at meals and ask impertinent questions, volunteer unsolicited information about themselves, suggest drinks and participation in social events, come face to face with you around every corner and appear from nowhere at your elbow when you are leaning on the rail in even the most secluded and wind-battered corner of the ship. Even these, however, swim and dissolve before your eyes; they are no less importunate than they would be on land, but they are less real: they are travelling sometimes for bizarre purposes, such as to jettison the ashes of their loved ones in mid-ocean. It is all very bad for the equilibrium, and for days after you step ashore the decks continue to move under your feet.

So much for travel. When I returned to Scotland I determined to seek work, a self-sufficient and meaningless work with no purpose outside itself, and at a good distance from Edinburgh. I have always despised the general acceptance of the concept of work as a social obligation, or as a necessity for the moral well-being of the individual. I sought work now only to take the place of the spiritual and intellectual life which had effectively ceased for me since my release from prison; and as something made necessary only by that lack. Work would have to become my life, for a time at any rate, work purely for its own sake, and I would embrace it whole-heartedly. For mental or physical laziness had never played any part in my hatred of work; I hated it only insofar as it stood in the way of things more important than itself. Now that these conditions pertained no longer I was more than happy to work. Accordingly I presented myself at the employment exchange; I found myself one of those sly, humiliated men who sit for hours daily on hard benches, suppliant and unprotesting, while civil servants walk away with files in their hands and consult their colleagues on endless matters of disturbing and hidden moment. This atmosphere I found strangely sympathetic: it is a measure of how much I had changed during the preceding months, that I felt no trace of impatience, that I could even with equanimity permit people to jump the queue in front of me. I had time at my disposal, after all, time without limit and little else. As it turned out it was several weeks before anything suitable presented itself: but at last I was offered the post of kitchen hand at the Salachy Hotel in Speyside, where I am now: a small establishment which has recently been encouraged, by the beginning of the development of ski-ing in the area, to stay open during the winter season. This job I gladly accepted, and set out at once for the north. And my life, these days, has a certain serenity.

Yes, my life has a certain serenity these days, a fine simplicity. I might have said repose, but that would suggest physical ease. Off season my work is in fact quite light, but I have discovered that I actually like hard work anyway, when it is clearly delineated and requires nothing but physical application. During a busy time I am up about a quarter to seven, and at work by half past. It must be admitted that my toil is menial. I peel potatoes, scrub and prepare vegetables, grate cheese, empty rubbish. I wash dishes, scour pots, colanders, soup tureens and a wide variety of other kitchen receptacles and implements. Twice a week I scrub the kitchen floor. I keep the place clean and well-ordered, so far as is possible, though this is uphill work. Yet I can state plainly that I like my work; and because I am an intelligent man I am a good man at my job, very thorough, yet quite fast. Because I think fast and never do two jobs at once I never let chaos take over around me. Everything I have cleaned I dry as quickly as possible, and everything I have dried I return to its apppointed place. These are no mean virtues in a kitchen hand.

So for me there is the daily sustenance of that grand old reward, the joy and satisfaction of a job well done. Work and work alone gives form to my life nowadays; I have neither time nor desire to question its further justification. Its routine fills me with a dull contentment. On the other hand I do not claim for such work any deeper significance. In my more theoretical days, for instance, I might have said that the humblest work can become a creative act when it is done for its own sake in the light of the Eternal: Karma, the way of work. 'Greater is thine own work, even if this be humble, than the work of another, even if this be great.' Which is true: only I am at last practising humility, I who have ruined my life through the most violent pride; but I could be answered that I am doing nothing of the sort, that I am merely indulging a perverted desire to humiliate myself, that my pride is indeed ranker than ever. But the truth of the matter is that I no longer care in the slightest to determine the answers to such questions, I merely continue as I am.

I am happy in my work then, on the whole, and my leisure too is pleasant because there is comparatively little of it and I follow my inclinations entirely in my use of it, something I'm not yet accustomed to. Broadly speaking the only thing I do during my off-duty hours is walk. I get two or three hours off every afternoon and irrespective of climatic conditions I walk home and muse. Before I came here I used to think while I walked, but now I only muse. On my whole day off, too, I invariably walk, not to observe the beauties of my native land, though I often do this with pleasure, nor to keep exercised, though it has this effect, but because I like walking. My room is quite pleasant; it is small and plain of course, and the window looks out slap onto the side of a steep pine-covered hill which rises very close behind the house, so there are no panoramic views to distract me. I had trouble with the window when I first arrived—the snib was jammed and the joiner could not be got hold of at once; life is purgatory to me without fresh air, and though it was bitterly cold at the time I had a rough few days; but that trouble is all behind me now and if I am to dwell on the sorrows of the past such an incident must pale into insignificance, as they say, beside the life I led before I came to the Salachy Hotel. In the evenings I still read occasionally, but not often, it has never done me much good. And before I go to bed I intend to keep scribbling at these notes from time to time.

As for human contact, the necessity for it here is mercifully limited: I would not yet be up to it. Nor that human contact is something for which I have ever greatly cared. I have been accused, indeed, of misanthropy, but that is not quite right. No, I hate not people in general but only most people in particular. Here, at any rate, the staff are few: they lead their lives and I lead mine. The guests are more of a nuisance, the English tourists among them in particular, and as the summer season gets under way this situation is likely to worsen. Often while standing at the sink I hear their denatured voices wafting through the open windoe: 'Aoh look Fred, ther's an 'aggis!' 'W'ere then? Is it wearing a kilt, then?' It is true that many of my own countrymen are in their own way equally repellent. Their way of being repellent, however, is the one I prefer. But my contact with the guests is happily minimal. It affords me a little amusement, even, to observe the pitiful pleasure derived by such people from being in a position to patronise me, on the few occasions when our paths cross. The chambermaid tells me that often they smoke in bed. After coition, perhaps, stripped to the waist, as in films they have seen. If there is one thing I cannot abide it is smoking in one's bed. To copulate there is bad enough, but to smoke exceeds the limits of decency. A minor but persistent drawback of living in a hotel is the distressing thought, as you are lying in your bed, of all the copulation that may be going on round about you. It is not as if the guests were young, that would be all right, but most of them are middle-aged. It is the mass quality of the thing, all of them going at it at once, which is so bad; much worse of course in a big hotel, I couldn't stand that for long. It worries me, this thought, worries me. My attitude to sex is perhaps not altogether healthy. At times when I was young, for instance, I felt it as a matter of acute shame that I was the product of an impulse of sexual desire, however transient, and that everyone must realise this, should they ever chance to think about it, however unlikely that eventuality might be. An incapacitating attitude.

Three months now I have been at the Salachy Hotel: it is spring, and I am almost growing happy. Watching the bursting of life about me it occurs to me that one day, perhaps, I shall myself attempt to live again. I have this great advantage now, that I no longer hope. When you hope for nothing from a thing you cannot fear its failure, and if you do not fear failure you have nothing to lose by action. Lack of hope is the clue to the nature of my whole existence in this place: I have relinquished my claims upon anything beyond it, upon any other future for myself and upon any human being other than myself. I could lead this life with holiness, it is true, only a small but decisive inner turn would be necessary, but I can't, or don't want to, I have closed up my nature. For I have beaten my head against the hard wall of reality, which would not countenance my high desire. A repose that ever is the same, that is what I want the Salachy Hotel to remain for me now. It is not the silence that I wanted, the silence that has been earned, but nonetheless it is a silence and I am prepared to fight for it. To fight? What I have said cannot be entirely true, then, I have not completely shaken free of the old life, of the old pulls of aspirations, hopes, fears, affections and the love of truth.

To each man his own guilt: so to me, mine. From whatever sources I have drawn that guilt the responsibility lies with me alone: collective guilt being a lie. I accept what is mine, then, and only what is mine. For the man who refuses, at last, to bear the burden of what he is, forfeits the right to think, or act, or live. And my burden and my guilt consist in this: that I have within me a burrowing beast.

I do not know this beast, I do not control it, yet it is mine. But I am coming to know it. It has lain restrainedly, watchfully, its animation suspended, these five months I have spent at the Salachy Hotel, dedicated to a morose and degrading work, but just recently I have felt again its tentative stirrings, its first delicate exploratory proddings somewhere deep within me. Now, suddenly, I am on its trail. Its stronghold is unfathomably deep from which it burrows systematically, comprehensively, in all directions. How it entered my being I do not know, through one of the five narrow doorways of the senses perhaps; or whether it was not rather always there, locked within me at the moment of conception. Certainly I cannot, now that I have given it a substance by apprehending it, remember a time when it was not with me, nor one when I did not feel for it a secretive love. I suspect I came to love it first in my early childhood when it fashioned me a dwelling-place, the divine pleasure-garden of the autonomous will: cunningly it established itself thus as my resourceful ally in my struggle with recalcitrant reality. It concealed from me that its purposes were always its own, that like a cancer within me it was foreign and an enemy to my good. Thenceforth, unwittingly, I played the collaborator.

Unrestingly it has pursued its opaque and undeviating ends, growing all the time in strength and in stature, nourishing itself unceasingly upon my nature, taking over and assimilating to itself ever more of my spiritual structure. Until now at last like an incubus it has entered stealthily into my virtues, converting and transmuting them to its own calm and unknowable logic. It entered, at a stroke, the precious faculty of the will, diverted it, perverted it. That has been its profoundest work, the key to its dominion over the virtues; and from there it has reached at last to my clear love of truth, and made that an enemy to love of my neighbour. And I have co-operated, what is worse, in this control of my virtues, for an ignoble reason: that is, by willing my self-assertion in the name of truth and principle I have sought to keep at arm's length deeper truths and mysteries which I unconsciously feared would destroy me if I were to stumble some day unawares upon their meaning.

So my struggle now must be to free my virtues from the dominion of the burrowing beast, to seek with every resource at my command to reduce its territory within me until at last it is driven out, or walled up at least within its irreducible stronghold. I have indeed only one resource as yet against it, but is is the most useful one, the resource of understanding, of knowledge, of intelligence. I must come to understand the instincts of this blind, burrowing thing, train myself to anticipate its directions, lie in wait for it and perhaps ambush it somewhere along its devious path. It is a guerrilla war I must wage against this enemy within the gates, a slow intractable war of attrition. Armed with understanding and an impossible resilence I gather myself together for this task.

After tonight I do not expect to make any further entries in this journal. The phase of my life which gave it its purpose is nearly done, I believe, and the preoccupations which informed it are played out, or transformed into something other. To prolong it would be both arbitrary and unproductive. I look to the falling away of mentality and will; I think I can see, at a great distance and by straining my eyes very sedulously, the approach of a time when other things will have their day.

Today I was free from work, and I decided to walk up the Lairig Ghru to the Pools of Dee. Kind Fortune favoured me with an exceedingly propitious day, clear and nippy early, for we are well into the second half of September, yet with a promise of heat to come. I set out before eight, and walked along the road towards Coylumbridge. The hard clarity of the light and the sharp pungency of the morning atmosphere filled me with exhilaration; the dark, gouged-out gap of the Lairig invited my penetration, the mountains' massive bulk challenged my mastery. I was struck by the omnipresent complexity of the spiders' webs, heavy and glistening with dew, which completely swathed the heather and dominated the immediate surroundings; another hour or two and they would be quite invisible again, the innumerable indefatigable creators leaving no more decisive impact upon what we think of as the human world. Yet how they must constantly teem there about our feet!

It was chilly as I started walking up the course of the burn, and I walked briskly. Walking is my original and most enduring love; yet today's expedition presented the strongest sort of contract to my customary walking trips from home, in the Pentlands. I used to love to do the long Pentland walks, crossing the hills from Balerno to Carlops, or from the Lanark Road to West Linton by the Cauldstaneslap. I was always by myself, solitary and glad to be so, choosing a weekday to lessen the change of meeting anyone on the way, so that when I got up into the hills I could shout and sing and talk to myself, and if I came to a boggy patch bound crazily from tuft to tuft like one possessed. A clear, bracing day in October was my favourite choice, with perhaps a fresh breeze blowing, a day which, unlike today, would never become hot; or a lightly-clouded day of weak sunshine in early spring. These were the hills of home, to me as to Stevenson, not much richness or majesty of scenery as up here, hills bare, bleak and obdurate, yet when you knew them well, subtle and varied in their character, possessed of different shades and tones and of innumerable meanings; and above all, mine. From their vantage points I could enter into imaginative possession of my country, there was no part of Scotland to which from there I could not turn my eye or the further-penetrating eye of my mind. To the north-east lay the stark, noble outline of my city, with its familiar and beloved hinterlands, to the east and a little to the south the chain of the Lammermuirs when my people came, and beyond them the North Sea; southwards the Border hills rolling out of sight; north-west the central plain, with the orange slag-heaps of the dead shale pits in the middle distance, beyond them the Ochils and the Campsies, and on a very clear day Ben Lomond or Ben Ledi representing the expanses of the Highlands which they guarded; then round again to the placid hills of Fife beyond the grey-blue sliver of the Forth. And just below me a landmark which has always held for me a strange attraction, the blunt protruberance of Dalmahoy Hill whence, it was once said, Mynyddawg and Gwlyged led the ill-fated men of Gododdin, still drunk from their year-long feast of mead, on their last long march to Catraeth against the Saxon. Such was the moral force which these scenes engendered that my walks were never just walks for me, they were heady draughts of cold, exultant idealism; the chilly flame of my future and my destiny would burst out in my head, kindled by the raw mental violence of my youth. Thus would I cross the hills. Crossing the hills, narrow though the range is, always held for me a powerful, non-conceptual, almost mystic meaning, which I took to be an ancestral inheritance. I was never tired when I got to the other side, even though my feet might hurt, I wanted to walk on and on, to cross further range after range. To turn back semed a meaningless failure. Humanity was foreign to the spirit of these hills: the cold, the hard, the noble, the reticent, the ideal, these were the spiritual forces native to them, and it was to find these, and to know their correspondence with my own soul, that I went up into the hills.

Today was quite different. I was just a human being on a day's walking expedition with a clear objective, one of probably many people who would be doing the same thing in the same place this weekend. As the day wore on it became hot, sweaty work, requiring considerable concentration, and an effort which looked for a reward of final achievement and refreshment. The splendour of the scenery and the richness and variety of the natural order around me impressed themselves upon my senses, as themselves and nothing more. My mind remained thoroughly engaged with the task on hand, and the country through which I travelled demanded that it should be so. The task on hand was simply the difficult and tiring, but, it was to be hoped, rewarding ascent of a mountain pass, the movement ever upwards and inwards into greater contact with the mountains, more intimate grappling with the physical substance of the earth. No wide vistas opened up before me with ideal and extending suggestions: I was not even going through the pass into a new country, I would have to turn back at the summit towards the familiar parts from which I had come. Everything in my path was concrete and specific, good and wholesome work to be done with the literal sweat of the brow to prove it. Sensual pleasure was what I sought.

For the first stretch of the journey I could see the great handsome cleft of the pass far ahead, seeming a great way off, with nearer at hand and a bit to the right the sugar-loaf of Carn Eilrig, my changing relation to which would give me some indication of my progress. By the time I reached the iron bridge the chill of the morning had left the air, though my feet were still soaked with dew, and I began to warm up. I had hoped to be among the first to set out upon the trek but on the long open stretch beyond the bridge I saw two figures tramping through the heather a long way off, too far to distinguish even their age or sex. It soon became clear however that I was making up on them quite fast, and this worried me a little, for I would have to pass them, and perhaps talk.

I entered thick pinewoods around the fork off to Loch Morlich, and began climbing. A luscious extravaganza of blaeberries on both sides of the path and stretching away in all directions gave me an excuse to pause for ten minutes and let my fellow-walkers get further ahead. They were much more professionally equipped than myself, with packs and climbing boots; I could see now that both were men of about my own age, one of them ginger-bearded. When I became tired of picking the small never-ending berries I set out again, with purple hands and mouth, up through the trees over a path which was difficult going because of the gnarled roots which everywhere crossed it. Emerging eventually from the woods into the open country again I found the Lairig opening up vast and splendid before me. The two ahead were taking a rest in the heather at the side of the path; they smiled and nodded reservedly as I passed them and I returned this greeting. The sun had now become very hot and the sky was brilliant. I was about level with Carn Eilrig; below to the right the burn sparked in the depths of an immense and steep gorge, and the sight made me very thirsty. In my duffle-bag I had lime juice in a silver flask, which I was waiting to mix with water from one of the many small and ice-cold burns which would soon be crossing the path. I was at the mouth of the pass proper now, the open ground on the left giving way to the first steep side of the mountains. I pressed on hard, climbing steadily though not steeply; I had still a long way to go, and was anxious to get to grips with the Lairig. Before long, though, I made a halt at a burn, drank, took off my shoes and socks and bathed my feet, taking pleasure in the initital shock of the icy water, and splashed my face.

About midday I was faced with a dilemma: the main stream and the path rejoined each other, but the path then forked, one prong continuing alongside the burn and the other pursuing a ridge about it. I was uncertain which to take. The way by the water seemed more pleasant so I chose that, deciding that it would be all the same in the end anyway. The two men were now in sight again some way behind. The little glen formed by the burn seemed altogether on a smaller scale than the surrounding grandeurs, more homely, like a Border glen. I came soon to a sort of lagoon with a large flat heather-covered space spreading away from it, and here I decided to rest and eat my sandwiches. After eating rapidly I looked about me and saw that the path I had chosen was obviously going to peter out; above me I saw walking along the ridge in single file a group of about six people and two dogs, who must have joined the path from some other route, for there had been no sign of them behind me and the two men had not yet appeared. I waited until they had got a good way ahead then began to clamber up the very steep slope to the top of the ridge, having to veer and tack in order to keep any kind of a footing. When I reached the top I found that I had accidentally timed it to coincide exactly with the arrival of the two men.

'You come up the hard way,' said the bearded one, grinning, and thus was the ice broken.

So I walked on in company with them, and in the event was glad enough to have them with me. They came from Dundee, they said, and went hill-walking almost every weekend during the summer. They had been right through the Lairig thirty or forty times, and never tired of it. The beard, who did most of the talking, spoke such a thick Scots that I had some difficulty in understanding everything he said, which didn't matter, for after a time his conversation settled down into an endless series of variations on a single theme, the pints they were going to have when they reached Braemar, and which he claimed were going to be over their throats before they were drawn, before they were ordered even, so great would be their thirst. The brilliant, tortuous elaborations he went into on this grand theme were in the finest tradition of Celtic art; I listened amazed and delighted. There was a ferocious extravagance, an exuberant joy in his pursuit of this single idea, which at first sight might have seemed capable of supporting little more than a passing joke. And when at last even he appeared to have exhausted this rich vein, he passed on to a related theme, namely the horrible possibility of their reaching Braemar after closing-time; though barring broken ankles or collapse from exhaustion, this was almost inconceivable. It was only the increasing difficulties of the terrain over which we were passing, which called for a good deal of concentration and effort, which finally forced him into silence.

As we continued to ascend the scenery had become increasingly bleak, rocky and desolate, and the weather too had changed. We were coming up towards the mists which almost always shroud the upper slopes of Ben Macdhui: grey clouds had blotted out the sun, and the air had become chilly and very damp. The path was now very rocky and hard on the feet; the abundance of stones everywhere had tempted people to build up an unnecessary number of cairns along its side. On our left was the great precipitous black scree which sheers down from Lurcher's Crag. I thought uneasily of the Grey Man. A depression had settled on us all to which none would probably have admitted; apart from the effort involved nobody felt like talking any more.

'We coulda been in wur beds,' observed the beard once; that was all.

Towards the summit the landscape became even bleaker and greyer, the stones under our feet growing increasingly larger until the path became lost in a vast waste of boulders which strewed the entire floor of the pass. I would have liked to understand how such a place was formed. It was a frustrating and irritating progress, jumping in an ungainly manner from rock to rock. It seemed pointless, too; for when the Pools of Dee finally came into view they were only cold, dank ponds amid the boulders; and beyond them, boulders stretching on into the distance. It was an end of the world sort of place altogether. I would have liked to have turned back before reaching even the first pool, but that would have been a shameful defeat, because although there was nothing to them, they had nonetheless been my objective all along: if you were doing the Lairig you just had to reach the Pools of Dee, that was all. But the first pool counted. There I said goodbye to my companions and wished them enjoyable pints, and stood for a time watching them trudging on doggedly through the boulders. Then I turned round and trudged back over my own. I was chilled to the marrow by now, and more than anxious to get away from this depressing place. The clouds were thick overhead and the damp seemed to be emanating from within my very bones; but when I reached the point where it was possible to look down over the coming descent I saw that I would soon be entering the heat and light once more, for this was only the resident weather of the summit of the pass. I was meeting quite a few people coming in the other direction by now, who must have set out about an hour later than myself. Several of them stopped and asked how far it was to the Pools of Dee; they seemed anxious to talk and prolong human intercourse, as if they were reluctant to press on into the chilliness before them. I was very glad to be going in the opposite direction. As I went on down, and the boulders gave way to stones and loose dirt, the harshness of the air relented and the warmth returned a little to my body; then before long I was walking again on a comfortable path through the heather, with friendly little burns crossing in front of me, and I realised that I was in the pleasant heat of the sunshine once more, though it had lost its midday power. It was strange to think that this place had remained warm and inviting while I had been struggling up through the bleak grey damp to the aridity of the summit.

As I moved further down into the friendly, familiar world of heat and beauty my spirits quickly revived, though I was tired by now and my feet hurt. I was glad to meet people and greeted them with friendliness, even high spirits. It was a long walk back down through the pine woods and over the heather to the iron bridge, and the last stretch back to Coylumbridge was unexpectedly protracted, but the day was beautiful and the atmosphere soft by now, and my tiredness was of the pleasant kind. A feeling of solidity and serenity had slowly been gathering strength within me as I came down: I knew that it would be possible for me to enter life again, however painfully. I thought of the grim spiritual journey which I had been making for a year or more, driven by my will towards a goal which I perceived only dimly and whose nature I might never understand. I had reached only a grey, arid death of the spirit, in which for a time I had thought with grim relish to rest content. The death-like life which I tried to lead at the Salachy Hotel was an easy way out, an attempt to simplify recalcitrant complexities, nullify them by a crude movement of the soul. From this barrenness it was now necessary for me to clamber down into some sort of life again. Not that I could forsee for myself any peaceful haven, nor for my problems any easy solution. Easy solutions were a lie, that I had discovered. I knew that to re-enter humanity would mean for me new obligations and struggles and much vile and obscure suffering. Yet it is better to live painfully than to be dead. I am beginning, at least, to be able to laugh at myself as heartily as I have always laughed at others; which is a start. 'You who aspire to greatness,' said Zarathustra, 'learn how to laugh!' Yes; but learn, too, in what *tone* to laugh.

As I passed down by the burn, I was in a sufficiently indulgent mood to smile and say 'Good afternoon' to a noisy group of English picnicers who were occupying a spot which had been dear to me since my childhood; but the ugly caravan site at Coylumbridge struck me with a sudden heavy depression. Then as I walked down the road towards Rothiemurchus I caught sight on my right of a monstrous hotel going up, and I was smitten with a sharp pain, a sudden violent return of the old anger, loathing and disgust. Already the brutal scars of development had begun their disfigurement of the Highland face; into this strong proud country which had maintained its integrity so long, the subtle hordes would enter unopposed. I understood then that I had my old self to bear and battle with yet, for which I would need every available resource, and the old unredeemed world to come to terms with still. I understood, too, that this world on which the sun shone so brightly today was in no sense mine; that the sun shone upon a world that was the seer's, and the soldier's and the judge's, as it has always been, and always will be, while it endures.

PAGAN'S PILGRIMAGE

I

CHILDHOOD AND YOUTH

My imagination has been haunted by the wrinkled-nosed laundryman for as long as I can remember. He was a sallow, bad-tempered and laconic fellow, who used to collect and deliver the laundry at our house, and he had a wrinkled nose. I was frightened of him, but also fascinated by him; he wore a uniform, and this marked him out for me as one having authority, so that I became to believe that this sinister character had powers to remove me from parental control and place me under durance. I used to loiter around the front door when he called, however, partially concealed behind my mother's skirts, flirting with danger. As well as a uniform, I remember, he had a leather satchel in which he kept his change. Whenever I misbehaved—threw my little sister's dolls on the fire, wet my bed or plunged my granny's six-inch hat-pin into the cat—my mother used to say, 'The wrinkled-nosed laundryman will get you.' You should not say things like that to a child. If you do, he, or she, may grow up with deep, unconscious fears: say, that the wrinkled-nosed laundryman will get him, or her. So it has been with me. I remain terrified of wrinkled-nosed laundrymen, to this day, even though my reason assures me that I am in little danger from them.

The stress which I lay upon the wrinkled-nosed laundryman at this early stage in my recollections is not fortuitous, as later events in my narrative will make clear. A more immediate influence upon my development however was that of my father, the Rev. Cuthbert Pagan, whom I much resemble. He was a Scotch preacher of the old school, and a man of infinite hypocrisies. A crafty peasant from Sanquhar, he had a mind of weaving, tortuous illogicality and a sullen temper. He also had illusions of grandeur. On a famous occasion he discharged from the pulpit the following blasphemous catalogue of the prophets of God: 'Abraham, Isaac, Jacob, Joseph, Moses, Joshua, Samuel, Elijah, Elisha, Isaiah, Jeremiah, Ezekiel, John the Baptist, Christ!'—then, in quiet, subdued but penetrating tones—'and lastly, Christ's humble servant, Cuthbert Pagan.' My mother was a kindly, long-suffering soul, and if she had a fault it was that she instilled in me an ineradicable and perhaps unjustified mistrust of wrinkled-nosed laundrymen. I had an elder brother, who persecuted me, and a younger sister, whom I persecuted. Yes, we were a close-knit family, we Pagans: discord being an infinitely more compelling bond than harmony.

My schooling proceeded apace. We lived in a village on the outskirts of Edinburgh, which the advance of the city has since swallowed up; and after a year or so at the local school I was dispatched into town to attend a private establishment. I was a bright pupil, heartily loathed by my teachers, who no doubt sensed in me a superior spirit. While always maintaining towards them an unexceptionable politeness I made it clear that I regarded them as less than my equals, and this consciousness may perhaps have rankled in them. They could never pin anything on me, though, so their resentment could find no natural outlet, releasing itself only in meagre driblets, a sarcastic shaft here, a hostile glance there, only occasionally an overt slight. Such gestures I received with icy indifference.

My father was not really so totally unsympathetic a man as I may have seemed to imply. He was a man without doubts, however. To convey a little of the sort of person he was, or rather wasn't: he was not the sort of man who, if he were looking out of his study window at the newly-mown lawn, and a cardboard cylinder from the centre of a toilet-roll were suddenly thrown over his fence, would immediately think to himself, 'I wonder what my reaction would be if that cylinder were to get up off the grass and begin to walk towards me?' No, he would be much more likely to say, 'Litter bugs! Damned vandals!' or something of that nature. That gives some idea of his limitations. He had no self-criticism.

One asset which my father did possess was a good ear for music. When I was about eight years old he began to take me to orchestral concerts in the Usher Hall of a Friday evening. I had already acquired a precocious passion for classical music, and in the atmosphere of the great concert hall my experience of the music became a physical, sensual event. The ornate lighting, the great sweep of the tiers, the noble organ, even the plush corduroy of the seats—all had their effect on me. I would watch each group of instruments in turn, and be thrilled by their physical forms, their mellow contours: I wanted to run my hands over the bodies of the violas and cellos and to press my nostrils against their elegant scented wood. As I watched and listened, stroking the arms of my seat the while, a primitive sucking reflex would commence in my mouth, which I only much later came to realise was the same action with which I had once drawn the milk from my mother's breasts.

I had soon mapped out a future for myself as a composer, and spent most of my free time covering sheets of expensive manuscript paper with unperformable compositions, meaningless arrays of notes which I believed to be masterpieces, created by a magic act of will, through which strenuous desire was able to compensate for the knowledge which I was aware I did not possess. I bought the Pelican *Lives of the Great Composers*, in three volumes, and imagined my own life as it would some day be chronicled in the fourth.

Unfortunately I had extraordinarily little musical ability, and was never able to learn so much as to sight-read. My fingers, too, were abnormally clumsy and unresponsive to my will. However I persisted with my piano lessons for many years. By the time I was in the senior school my progress had become so exceptionally slow and my performance so unremittingly hopeless that I began to harbour serious doubts as to whether

I had been wise in my choice of vocation. The idea caused me great mental torment. I had at that time a blind music teacher, a gentle creature of excessive sensitivity and a monumentally refined ear, to whom my endless incompetencies and barbaric discords were a source of something akin to physical agony. Often when I hit a wrong note he would draw his whole body together with a pitiful groan, and cast his sightless eyes up to heaven with a countenance blank with inexpressible suffering; on occasions the sweat would even break out on his brow. His passion afforded me a little comfort in my trouble, for already sadistic and masochistic impulses were jostling for supremacy in my soul. But really it was a bad time, as I came to face the irrevocable dissolution of my dreams. It is from this unhappy period that I date my thirst for the absolute, my yearning for some God-given, exalted destiny which would lift me far above the inherent limitations of my talents and personal attributes.

My father had destined me for the law, for which profession my brother Shugs was already preparing himself, and as the enforced abandonment of my compositional ambitions had left me without a purpose in life I went along with his desires for the time being. During my last year at school however my exemplary devotion to my studies was disrupted somewhat by a passion which I conceived for a skinny red-headed serving-wench in a low coffee dive called the Stockpot. I would spend most of my holidays and many of my evenings there, lingering over stale scones, feeding the juke-box and casting furtive glances at the object of my desires, who never evinced the slightest flicker of interest in my person and indeed seemed totally unaware of my attentions. My father somehow got to hear of my obsession, probably from a malicious schoolfellow of mine, and encouraged me to pursue my studies south of the border, where he doubtless hoped I might form some more salubrious attachment. I therefore proceeded in due course to — — — College, Cambridge, where my scholastic career was facilitated by the award of a Frank Proxmire Exhibition, of value £3 6s 8d per annum, an emolument ordinarily restricted to the younger sons of fishmongers residing within three miles of Norwich Cathedral, but that year magnanimously thrown open *pro hac vice*. But my heart remained at home in the Stockpot, and I benefited but little from the manifold advantages which proliferated about me for the taking in the gracious old city in the Fens. As soon as I came home for the Christmas vacation I headed straight for the Stockpot and remained ensconced there, more or less, for four weeks, without the least amelioration of my romantic affairs to show for my devotion. My only other current interest in life lay in tinkering with my motor-bike. I would tinker happily for four or five hours at a stretch, tuning and returning the engine to absolutely no practical purpose, revving and phutting away interminably in the manse garden, and roaring round and round the block emitting din and noxious fumes until our good neighbours were plagued beyond bearing, and began making fruitless representations to the minister, to whom my way of life was fast becoming a source of black-burning shame. As for myself, the aimlessness and vacuity of my existence was far from inhibiting my belief that heaven had marked me out for some high if yet undisclosed destiny, and my manner became saucy, overbearing and contemptuous beyond enduring.

One evening I returned home from the Stockpot to find a police car parked outside our front gate. I made my way quietly indoors, and tiptoeing up to the door of my father's study lent an ear to his conversation with the policeman. They were discussing me. It seemed that the neighbours, obtaining no satisfaction from my father who in truth was already quite unable to control me, had appealed to the law as the only hope of quelling my mechanical activities.

'I've done a' I can, officer, an' I can dae nae mair,' my father was saying, 'he's aye in yon Stockpot. I mind fine when he was a bairn, constable, he wouldnae wear his Claxton cap, an' see the lugs on him the day. I mind I said to my wife, I says we've a bad yin here, wife, I says, we've a young deil here, Mrs Pagan, that we hae.'

I slunk away in embarrassment on hearing this insulting

talk, and sought the peace of the dark garden to nurse my wounded pride; but after the policeman had gone I re-entered the hallway nonchalantly and with a lot of noise, whistling some mindless popular song of the day, and tossing my gauntlets and crash-helmet carelessly on a brass tray. As I hoped, my father emerged from his study pale with fury, with a half-written sermon still in his hand, and accosted me as I made as if to go up to my room.

'An' where hae *you* been, my fine young chap?' he hissed dangerously, savouring and caressing the words.

'In the Stockpot, father,' I replied with a resigned sigh.

'Stockpot, say ye? I'll gie ye Stockpot! It's the back o' my hand you'll be feelin', my jockie! There was nae Stockpot for me, I can tell ye, when I cam up frae Sanquhar forty year syne, for tae gang tae the college! Sixty mile I walked, in my bare feet! No, there was nae Stockpot for me, an' nae grants, but a puckle oatmeal in my pouch, an' bloody hard darg, an' a straw pallet to lay my banes on at the end o' the day. Stockpot, ye say? Out o' my sicht, ye bauchle, ye're nae son o' mine! Out o'my sicht, damn ye, ye're nae langer a Pagan!'

And he kept on, in this excessive way, until I became more than a little weary. All the time he was speaking my father was circling round me, leering and sniggering and making idiotic little springs backwards and forwards on his toes, attempting no doubt to torment me in a manner time-honoured amoung Scottish patriarchs. All this in a dog-collar. My mother and sister, meanwhile, were waiting and snivelling in the kitchen. It was a gruesome scene. I waited until he had quite finished and gave him a long, dispassionate look.

'Before my conception,' I said, 'when I was as yet but a profound idea forming in the mind of God, who would have imagined that you would be the instrument chosen for its realisation?'

My father was totally nonplussed by my outrageous audacity, and it was several seconds before he shouted 'Blasphemer!' and hurled his sermon at my head. Abandoning it where it lay scattered copiously about the floor, he buried his face in his hands and fled sobbing into his study.

But I too was soon to taste for the first time of the cup of sorrow, for one day my love disappeared from the Stockpot, convicted of pilfering from the till. I had no idea where she might have gone and I never saw her again. I had never spoken to her other than to say, 'A cup of coffee and a soda scone, please,' nor had I ever learned her name. My failure however only drove me to over-compensate once again, and I became more than ever convinced that I was a person quite out of the ordinary run, whose day would dawn at last.

Shortly after this I went back to Cambridge, and did not return home for the Easter vacation; in an effort to forget my pain I turned towards the delights of erotic literature and the idle pleasures of the river. All that halcyon summer I spent lying in a punt near Grantchester, reading *Women in Love*, *Lolita* and *The Golden Ass* of Apuleius, and consuming cream and honey. Reeling under the effects of these gross stimuli, I performed miserably in my preliminary examination, failing even to obtain an allowance towards the Ordinary B.A. degree, and was sent down. A career in the law was now out of the question, and returning home in disgrace I was apprenticed to my uncle in the antiquarian bookselling firm of Bookless and Bone, Pitt Street.

II

BOOKLESS & BONE'S

My maternal uncle, Sean Bookless, was sole proprietor of this little business, Bone having departed some years before to the great knackery in the sky. Sean was a melancholy old fellow with a head rather like a rugby ball or a cantaloup melon set at an angle of forty-five degrees to his neck. He had an habitually resigned, apathetic look on his face, spoke but sparingly and then sadly, and suffered badly from the cold. I can see him now, seated in his little nest at the back of the shop, his knees pressed primly together, his womanish old hands outstretched towards a meagre oil heater, an immensely long pink college boating scarf wound innumerable times round his neck, a drop forming at the end of his nose. He was said to have resembled a gipsy in his youth, but I found this difficult to accept. Uncle Sean taught me all I know about the second-hand book trade, the only field in which I have ever attained even a modest eminence. I was not industrious, and the fact is that he had very little need of me, having an excellent assistant already in the shape of wee Tam Tudhope, of whom more anon. I had been employed mainly as a favour to my unhappy parents, and I was accordingly paid very little. That drawback was compensated for however by my access to the infinite riches of the books themselves.

Yes, my true education was received among the musty volumes of Bookless and Bone's bookshop. The shop specialised in theology, philosophy and eighteenth-century historical works, and had a good stock also of translations from classical literature.

Reading widely and deep, I soon succumbed to rampant atheism and worse, washing down Rousseau and Kant with great heady draughts of Schopenhauer, Nietzsche and Jean-Paul Sartre. I now disdained to enter the portals of my father's church, which I had always found a gloomy, depressing place. As a child I had positively dreaded my weekly visits there, chiefly because of a vague suspicion that the wrinkled-nosed laundryman lived within it: several times I imagined that I had caught sight of him lurking in one of its shadowy recesses. Now, my alienation was not merely intellectual; the very construct of the building caused in me a physical recoil, and appeared the heavy badge of an unwholesome truth, signifying something foul and shadowy in the very structure of the universe. My apostasy was the final straw for my father, and he banished me from the manse; I was allowed to rent a small flat above the bookshop, which had once been the home of Mr. Bone, but since his death had been used only for storage.

Of great importance to me at this time was the influence of wee Tam. Wee Tam was a socialist, as no one who knew him could possibly forget for long. He might not have had the advantage of much formal book-learning, but God, could he argue! He could. And did, boring everyone to rigidity and distraction with his interminable metaphors of chains, loaves of bread and so on. Few people minded about that, however, because Tam was such a good-hearted chap when all was said and done. On one afternoon a week his student girl-friend Jenny, or Jenny-lass as she was most frequently called, came in to relieve him in the shop. She too had a propensity for homespun dialectic and was constantly reiterating a few well-tried propositions with a good-natured imbecility that was hard to resist. Indeed I quite failed to resist it, not least perhaps since I was strongly attracted to Jenny, who was a fresh, well-covered, rosy-cheeked lass. They were a decent pair the two of them, solid and straightforward as you could wish, courageous and self-respecting, the very salt of the earth, and at their behest I read copiously in Marx, Engels and Lenin, and soon became a fiery armchair revolutionary. My brief sojourn in Cambridge had already left me a confirmed Scottish nationalist and I was now ripe for all kinds of radical departures.

I became good friends with wee Tam and Jenny-lass, and spent many a riotous evening at Tam's flat. He had quite a reputation in his circle as an amateur comedian, a reputation which was founded at bottom on the fact that his jokes were not at all funny. A typical example might run like this: This wife says to her man, Would you like a toasted tongue sandwich? Ay, he says. Well you cannae, she says, the dog's eaten them. Now no one who did not share Tam's particular sense of humour could find that in the slightest degree amusing. It was not that he found the concept of a toasted tongue sandwich extraordinary in itself, though others might; on the contrary Tam liked toasted tongue sandwiches and ate them often. Nor was there any hidden or metaphysical meaning in the joke, metaphysics lying quite outwith wee Tam's sphere of interests. It was just that Tam found it peculiarly funny that a wife should ask her husband if he would like a toasted tongue sandwich and then, when he said he would, tell him that the dog had eaten them. Consequently when he told such a story he would tell it with such confidence and gusto that no one listening to it could believe that it could really be as pointless and inane as it actually was. Everyone thought that they had missed the point, and no one likes to admit that he has missed the point of a joke, so they laughed heartily. Particularly if it was a joke like the one cited, concerning wives and dogs and tongues, they would begin to imagine that it was a vulgar innuendo which they had missed, and they would laugh exceptionally loudly for fear that they might be thought lacking in sexual experience or *savoir faire*. A spiteful character who was more self-confident than others, or a better actor, might say to his neighbour, 'You didnae see the point of that, did you?' And the neighbour would blush and mumble into his beer that of course he did. So when it was time to leave and they were staggering home together, the one thus humiliated would say to his companion (just to show that he really had

understood the joke, for otherwise how could he have had the
nerve to bring the subject up again?), 'Christ, that was a great
joke of wee Tam's about the toasted tongue sandwiches, I was
fair pissin' myself laughing at him!' Then he would repeat the
joke. And the other, who of course had really been in the same
boat himself all along, fearing now in his turn that he was all
alone in the world, would bellow anew with feigned laughter,
and his friend would join in, and before long they would both
be laughing from the heart from sheer relief that the danger
seemed to be past and the other no longer doubted that he
had seen the joke. Such a relief would it be indeed, that in no
time at all they really would be finding it excruciatingly funny
that a wife should ask her husband if he would like a toasted
tongue sandwich, then when he said he would, tell him that the
dog had eaten them. So often folk could be seen leaving Tam's
house falling about and holding on to each other, fair pissing
themselves in fact, and sometimes literally, with laughter at jokes
that weren't in reality in the slightest bit funny at all. It can be
said to his credit that in such ways wee Tam brought a measure
of what can only be called joy into not a few drab lives.

Into my own drab life however it was Jenny-lass rather than
wee Tam who brought for a brief time a measure, if not perhaps
of joy, then at least of solace. Since my painful experience of
the Stockpot era I had fought shy of women, and I affected in
the presence of Jenny a protective veneer of lofty indifference to
her attractions, although I often burned for her in my entrails.
It was probably this supposed indifference which inflamed her
with the itch to ensnare me; she no doubt regarded me as a
challenge, as in very truth I was. Her onslaught when it came
took me wholly by surprise. On the days when she worked in
the bookshop we were in the habit of going for a drink around
half-past five, where we would shortly be joined by wee Tam,
and an evening of innocent carousal would follow. What I had
not bargained for on this occasion was the absence of wee Tam
on a visit to his widowed mother at Easthouses, which precluded
his return before the following morning. It would be tedious

to relate, even if I remembered them, the progressive stages of the flirtation which ended with my finding myself, it seemed quite without my own volition, in bed with Jenny in my little attic above the premises of Bookless and Bone. There I drew her voluptuous flesh uncertainly towards my quaking frame.

'How fast your heart is beating!' Jenny exclaimed, biting my earlobe provocatively.

'It always does,' I said. This was true enough.

'As fast as this?' she whispered knowingly. She could have spoken normally, for so far as we were aware there was no one present but ourselves, but for some reason she chose to whisper. She might even have shouted, though I admit that that would have been quite as pointless as to whisper.

'Yes, just about, I think,' said I, and felt around for my pulse. After a spell of such badinage, it appeared that I was not doing what was expected of me.

'Women can come too, you know,' Jenny volunteered. I thought that her remark probably referred to a Burns Supper which was being organised at that time.

'Where to?' I asked, just to make sure. Jenny guffawed immoderately at that, I remember. I suppose she was justified. At any rate, she did succeed after a long and bitter struggle in getting me where she wanted me, and where I wanted to be, and I was almost excessively grateful. I had high hopes that this would be but the first of a long series of comparable encounters.

The following morning I was called into my Uncle Sean's little nest at the back of the shop. He paced up and down nervously for a minute or two, stopping every now and again to warm his hands at the oil-heater and deliver a wretched cliché about the weather, evidently finding difficulty in broaching some delicate topic.

'There are ghostly principles at work in this world,' he began at last, turning towards me boldly, 'and in their honouring men must live and die.' He was a prosy old devil.

'Do you follow my drift?' he asked in a stern manner when I made no reply.

'No, uncle,' I said, truthfully.

He sighed wearily. 'Then let me put it another way. There is a difference between right and wrong. Do you catch my meaning?'

'No, uncle'

'I see,' said Uncle Sean, after a charged silence, 'that I shall have to be brutally direct with you. I shall tell you something. When I was a young man it was my fervent desire to establish in writing the delineations of hell. I thought that if I could define and mark off the hell in which I lived, I could make of it something spatial and finite from which I could plan some day to make my escape. But as I grew older I discovered that hell expands in proportion to the expansion of life, that every joy carries with it its own hell. In those early days I was a stranger to the bodies of women and to the succour of their love and companionship. I was utterly alone. But this changed, life expanded for me in due course and in the fullness of time these things came to me—and the hell which they carry with them. It did not take me long to discover that one of the worst hells is the hell wrought by women.'

He paused at this point, to draw breath and to observe the effects of his impressive tirade. As I had not the remotest idea what he was talking about, he must have been disappointed; but nothing daunted, he launched forth once more, striding up and down with quite uncharacteristic energy and gesticulating in an italianate fashion as he spoke.

'Have you not noticed,' he pursued, 'that Woman speaks the language of the slave? Always, always. Do you want to be part of her cursed 'we'? Do you want to see the rest of humanity negated for your sake? Woman's love *negates* all on whom it does not rest. And win or lose, she takes everything from you, your manhood, your pride, above all your holy singleness. For Woman's slavery debases Man. You can escape the taint of this debasement only by abjuring your own tyranny, for until Woman's nature is changed, Man can only play the tyrant. Only by Man's forswearing Woman, then, can she be led out of her slavery. But if this altruistic motive has no appeal for you, then I appeal to your self-preservation. Turn away from Woman if you want to survive.'

The lamentable harangue was at an end. Now that he had said his piece, all the wind seemed to depart from out of my uncle's sails, and he deflated like a pricked balloon. Probably he realised that he had made a fool of himself.

'Do you see what I'm driving at?' he ventured almost beseechingly.

'No, uncle,' I persisted heartlessly, and in tones of icy contempt. He could beat about the bush no longer.

'Stop messing about with Jenny-lass,' he mumbled quickly, looking away from me in embarrassment as he did so and fiddling around with objects on his desk in a pitiful attempt to cover his confusion.

'But, uncle...' I began, before I could stop myself. I knew at once that I had made a grave mistake, for this moment of weakness restored to him at a stroke his lost advantage over me.

'Not a word!' he proclaimed imperiously, swinging around full of confidence, fixing me with a stern eye, and putting forth the palm of his hand in the gesture of a policeman halting traffic. 'Your protests are of no avail. It happens that I came into the shop late last night to go over the accounts, and was disturbed by the sounds of your lewd embraces above me. Floors have ears, you know, as well as walls.' He smiled smugly, childishly gratified at having got his point over at last. In truth he had me just where he wanted me, and there was little I could do except hang my head abjectly. Uncle Sean was now completely puffed up with his petty triumph, and it was inevitable that he would overplay his hand.

'And your friend wee Tam, I dare say, is playing the complaisant lover?' he asked with malicious sarcasm, watching me closely to revel in the discomfiture which he hoped this shaft would produce.

'No,' I replied absolutely tonelessly, in the way of imparting a purely factual piece of information, and without betraying a flicker of either resentment or apprehension. I revelled in such psychological warfare, and to stonewall my uncle's ego-aggression in this way gave me a huge and insolent sense of inner strength.

Uncle Sean was visibly put out by my cool handling of the situation, and was betrayed into a too hasty riposte.

'I sometimes think there is a nasty streak in you somewhere, Horatio!' he exclaimed in irritation, quite losing his *sang-froid*.

I did not deign to reply, and Uncle Sean must have realised that he would suffer further humiliating reverses if he were to persist in his cruel attempt to bait and belittle me. He directed towards me a generous open smile, as if to indicate that between men of good will hard words could be exchanged on both sides without leaving a residue of ill-feeling or leading to any loss of mutual respect. He then dismissed me with an airy wave of the hand.

'Go,' he said, 'and sin no more'; falling into blasphemy in his efforts to end the interview on a note of urbane magnanimity.

I went; and was given no opportunity to sin any more, not at least by Jenny.

III

THE MYSTERIOUS STRANGER

I was highly delighted by the outcome of this tête-à-tête, and felt a surge of restless self-confidence flow through my veins. In fact I was getting to be delighted with myself a good deal of the time these days. More and more I felt myself to be a superior being, and experienced dissatisfaction only in that I could think of no suitable way in which to exercise this superiority. In particular I believed that unlike the rest of humanity, or ninety-nine per cent of them, I was uniquely favoured in the possession of a hard core at the centre of my being. Those unfortunates, I was convinced, who were capable of coping with life more effectively and with greater decisiveness than myself, were handicapped by the Almighty in being constructed in their central regions of a sweet, inchoate, syrupy substance which would inevitably discharge itself at the moment of crisis. With myself, on the other hand, though there were admittedly layers and layers of weakness from the surface inwards, which you could go on stripping off almost endlessly as though peeling an onion, at the very centre there lay a pure, immalleable, irreducible core, of adamantine properties. I was extremely proud of this useful piece of equipment, and dying to put it to use. Clearly, I was intended for some destiny quite out of the common range, and I waited with great impatience for this to reveal itself.

It happened that one day a consignment of books arrived in the shop which bore the legend 'Ex Libris Sykes-Buffington' on a label pasted within. The label bore also a highly elaborate coat-of-arms embodying I cannot remember what impressive heraldic devices. When I showed this casually to wee Tam the effect was quite extraordinary. He turned purple in the face, spat on the floor, and emitted oaths which left me in no doubt that he did not hold the Sykes-Buffington clan in high esteem. When he had recovered a little he managed to tell me that this striking appelation was the family name of the Viscount Gadarene, a gentleman who appeared to occupy a position of some prominence in Tam's demonic pantheon. Anthony Augustus d'Arcy Thystletone-Medici-Fanshawe Shoolbread Blockheid Sykes-Buffington, 14th Viscount Gadarene, was not, I learned, an ordinary, flesh-and-blood mortal like you and I. He did not, like you and I, labour day in and day out in a second-hand bookshop to earn a meagre pittance with which to buy his daily bread. He did not take the bus to work in the morning or have a pie and chips for his tea or enjoy a few pints on a Friday night or go to see Hibs play Rangers on a Saturday. He did not live in a council house and worry constantly about where the next instalment on the TV was coming from, nor did he spend many of his holidays at Butlin's in Ayr. Ho no. Not Anthony Augustus. Anthony Augustus owned, among other things, fifty thousand acres of a Hebridean island, but you would not find him very often at Teuchtershards, his Highland seat. Only, in fact, during the grouse-shooting season, or perhaps on the odd weekend when he might feel like flying up to kill a few stags. At other times you would be more likely to track him down to Bermuda, or his villa in the south of France, or his modest mansion in Wales, or perhaps to Pratt's or Boodle's, his London clubs—unless, of course, he happened to be at a board meeting of one of the eleven private and public companies of which he was a director. But in all likelihood he would be voting by proxy. The 14th Viscount Gadarene did most things by proxy. For this product of Winchester and New College, Oxford, naturally had flunkies everywhere eager to do his bidding; unless it was bidding for shares in some exploitative venture, in which case he would be unlikely to entrust his hard-earned pennies to anyone with less impressive credentials than his London stockbroker.

I was naturally highly enraged by this information. A powerful hatred, as was only proper, began to seethe within me for this execrable parasite, an emotion which the passage of days and weeks did not diminish but enlarged. Dwelling constantly on the enormity of his offence as I hung idly around during the many weary hours when there was little doing in the bookshop, I began to harbour for Lord Gadarene sentiments little short of murderous, and gleefully looked forward to the day when he and his like would be swept for ever from the earth. That day, alas, seemed still to be hopelessly far distant, for those who were most enraged by the existence of the Sykes-Buffingtons of this world always had a bark that was measurably worse than their bite. People like wee Tam might scream and stamp and shout but they were not capable of taking any positive action to make an end of the enemy. Why? Because they had soft centres, undoubtedly; only somebody like myself, someone with an incontestably hard centre, might be able to achieve something in this direction. My heart swelled proudly as this lofty thought entered my consciousness. Some embryonic sense of my purpose in life was at last beginning to take shape within me. In the weeks that followed, it slowly attained greater distinctiveness of form, and a more substantial life. A seed had been planted which was to grow into a monster.

I had further matter to brood upon at that time. My erotic life was once again not going well. It had not occurred to my vanity that Jenny-lass might prefer not to repeat the experiment which had given rise to my Uncle Sean's formidable lecture. Not only was she apparently far from wishing to repeat it, she was not even willing to acknowledge by word or sign that it had ever taken place. It did not escape my attention that she took the greatest care never in any circumstances to be left alone with me. On the afternoons when she worked in the bookshop she always seemed to manage to get Uncle Sean to spend most of his time in the front shop, which he did rarely in the normal course of events; and if anything positively obliged him to remain in his nest she usually contrived to get sent out on a message. Failing that, she would make a telephone call, generally to wee

Tam, which was especially galling. Before long I was absolutely convinced that Jenny was in collusion with Uncle Sean in this matter. What particularly infuriated me was the smug pleasure which my uncle clearly derived from the situation, and I determined to find the first possible opportunity to humiliate the old jessie. In the presence of wee Tam, Jenny was often decidely cool to me, and I was further tormented by the possibility that she might have confessed to him the story of our brief and inelegant liason. Altogether I was deeply wounded. A pall of deepest gloom began to settle over me, and I could find relief from my misery only in occasional temper tantrums, which for some reason often came upon me in the middle of the night, when I would rise from my bed and rage around incontinently, overturning furniture, smashing crockery, ripping clothes and curtains to shreds, grovelling howling on the floor in a self-indulgent fashion, and generally wallowing in shameful self-pity. Such outlets dissipated only the most acute of my tensions.

One evening around this time, when the nights were drawing in and an autumnal darkness was in the air and seeping insidiously into the gloomy twilight which habitually prevailed in the drab premises of Bookless and Bone, a sinister-looking gentleman appeared in the bookshop, seemingly from nowhere. I did not hear him come in; I was alone in the shop at the time and had been rearranging some volumes in the theology section. I had turned away for a moment or two for some reason, and when I turned back again there he was standing half in shadow between two tall rows of shelves, and fixing me sternly with a black and glittering eye. I received a considerable shock, because at the first glance I took him to be myself. The resemblance was extraordinary; yet the image I saw was not that of myself as I then was, but as I might expect to be in twenty or thirty years' time. I was so astonished that I dropped a pile of books and stood staring helplessly at him for some moments, probably with my mouth open. The mysterious stranger said nothing for quite a time, but continued to scrutinise me with a scornful, satirical look on his face.

'I am sorry to have startled you,' he said at length, 'I keep forgetting how quiet I am in my approach.'

He smiled enigmatically, and I was suddenly reminded irresistibly of an expression which I had often seen distort the features of the wrinkle-nosed laundryman. I felt the sweat break out on my brow and for a moment I was afraid that I was about to faint.

'Can I be of any assistance to you?' I managed to stammer, pulling myself together with a great effort of will.

He took his eyes off me at last and cast them around the rows of volumes collecting dust on the endless shelves.

'Perhaps you can,' he said, as if half to himself, 'perhaps you can. I am looking for a very rare book and so far all my efforts have been unavailing. Is it too much to hope that I may be luckier here?'

'What is it called?' I asked helpfully.

'*Famous Assassins*,' he said, with a scornful smile playing about his lips, 'by E.V. Messer.'

I had to admit that I had never heard of the book, and I was certain that Bookless and Bone had no copy of it, for I was acquainted with virtually every volume in the shop, and regarded many of them almost as my old friends. The gentleman told me that the date of publication was 1946, and mentioned an imprint which again was unknown to me but which he said belonged to New York. I promised that I would make enquiries of my uncle when he returned from the dentist's, and asked whether I could have a note of the gentleman's address and phone number so that I could let him know any result. He refused to supply me with these, however, saying that he would call back in a few days' time.

'If, in the meantime, a copy should unexpectedly fall into your hands, I should be obliged if you would lay it aside for me,' he requested. 'My name is Raith: R-A-I-T-H.'

I replied that I would certainly do as he wished, though I thought the chances of a copy turning up were very remote indeed.

'Ah, you never can tell,' the mysterious fellow replied. 'Things have an odd way of turning up when you expect them least and need them most.' He gave me a quick, penetrating look and let out a short, ugly laugh, then turned abruptly and walked out of the shop, leaving me considerably unnerved.

When the following morning I gave an acount of this incident to Uncle Sean he was greatly puzzled, for both title and imprint meant as little to him as they had to me, and yet he was a walking catalogue of such matters. Judge of my astonishment, then, when, glancing at a row among the shelves which I had been arranging at the time the gentleman had called the previous evening. I saw the volume in question staring me in the face. I found it difficult to accept the evidence of my eyes: it could not possibly have escaped my notice previously, for it was in the wrong section and glaringly out of place among the theological works which surrounded it, and was besides of an unusual shape, very tall and narrow. My first reaction to this discovery was to assume that the stranger must somehow have put it there himself as some kind of a horrid and unaccountable practical joke; but on reflection I could not see how this was possible, for I had turned away from the shelves only very briefly before first catching sight of him, and thereafter he had never been out of my sight until he left. Moreover I had returned to my previous task after his departure, and it seemed out of the question that the book could have escaped my attention then.

Fascinated by this mystery, I began to glance through the book, and was quickly captivated by its contents. It had chapters on most of the famous assassins of history. Brutus for instance, and Charlotte Corday, and John Wilkes Booth; but it also dealt with a number of much less well-known figures of whose careers I had previously been ignorant, including especially many of the Russian political assassins of the century before the Revolution. What was unusual about the book, which was excellently and persuasively written, was the attitude which the author had adopted towards his grisly subject-matter. All the assassins without exception were held up for the reader's admiration as heroic personages who had taken it upon themselves to rid mankind of noxious tyrants, often at the cost of the supreme personal sacrifice. Much was made of the ills inflicted by the victims of these assassins, the absolute probity of whose motives was never for an instant called into question.

The thesis which the author erected upon the foundations of those men's lives and works seemed to me absolutely compelling. It amounted to nothing less than a full-blooded adoption of the concept of public assassination as a means of remedying the ills and injustices of society, which it claimed must finally be laid at the door not of systems but of individuals. The arguments which E.V. Messer assembled to support this position were especially persuasive. Collective guilt, he asserted, in the sense of a responsibility shared by the community as a whole for the acts of individuals, was a lie. However much any individual might be formed by his inheritance, upbringing and environment, and played upon by fate, in the last resort each must bear the responsibility for what he was, otherwise all claims to free will must inescapably be denied him. The attribution to 'systems' of the blame for the evil acts of individuals was therefore meaningless, and the origins of the evils in human society must be sought solely in the wills of specific men and women, since only they possessed the powers of choice which pertained to free agents. The concept of systems which existed independent of the function of the individual will was therefore a mirage, and any belief in the reality of such a concept purely superstitious. It followed, then, Messer went on to argue, that remedies for society's ills must be sought at the level of individual action, which alone was meaningful, all else being merely an elaborate illusion. In many circumstances the only practical way of forestalling or turning aside the consequences of the wicked deeds of any particularly obnoxious individual would be to eliminate him, since to attempt to turn him from his bad ways by persuasion or argument would certainly be unrealistic. The book had apparently been written during the Second World War, and the example of Hitler was clearly in the forefront of the author's mind. He anticipated in a clever way the objections of those who would retort that the assassination of Hitler would have made but little difference to the course of history, since Hitler might be held only to have expressed or given form to a development in the consciousness of the German people as a whole. The German people as an entity did not exist, said Messer, the phrase representing only a collocation of individual Germans; and if this posited development of consciousness had taken place in the wills of a vast number of such individuals, all that was required to satisfy the terms of his argument was that *all* of these individuals should be eliminated.

I found that I could scarcely lay this book down, and at every available opportunity I was immersed in it, to the great neglect of my duties, and was called away from it by unavoidable business only with irritation and resentment. For some reason however I did not want wee Tam or my Uncle Sean to have any knowledge of my discovery, so I was at great pains to hide the book from their eyes at all times. I took it home with me that night and managed to devour the remainder without interruption. As its magnificent thought unfolded irresistibly and with splendour before my eyes, my consciousness was pervaded by a glorious feeling of lightness and freedom, as if I were experiencing reality immediately for the first time, having always up to this point received it distorted or obscured by the opacities of the deluded minds which had intervened between myself and the truth. I was infallibly persuaded that the reading of this book was to have a profound influence upon my future life, though so far I felt no curiosity to wonder how exactly this would come about.

The following evening I had volunteered to stay behind for a little after the shop closed, as my obsession with *Famous Assassins* had left me rather behind-hand with various tasks. I had more or less completed these and was about to depart when I heard a knock upon the locked glass door, and found the enigmatic Mr. Raith waiting to be admitted. I was about to launch forth about the miraculous appearance of the book he had been searching for when he forestalled me by asking me how I had enjoyed reading it. I was of course very astounded, but looking back upon it, perhaps not quite so astounded as I really ought to have been. Almost as soon as he had spoken I seemed to accept what he had said as more or less in the order of things, and besides I was so taken up with my enthusiasm for the contents of the volume that the manner of its arrival no longer seemed to matter very much. I waxed very loud in its praises, saying with truth that it had spoken more profoundly to my spirit than had all the Greek philosophers and modern idealists and materialists combined.

'Indeed', replied Mr. Raith (whose odd resemblance to myself had again struck me most forcibly), 'Messer's logic is compelling, and I have no doubt of the philosophical validity of his conclusions. The sad fact is, however, that they are most unlikely ever to be put into practice, because men of the stature required to undertake these assassinations in the spirit he recommends must necessarily be very rare birds.'

'But surely the deeds of those whom he cites have had the profoundest effects upon the course of history?' I was moved to protest.

'True,' said Raith with a cold smile, 'but yet very small compared with what would be possible if we had such men around in any abundance. The need for such great deeds—and the opportunities for them—can unhappily never be matched by a sufficiency of souls large enough to carry them through. A Brutus or a Lee Harvey Oswald is not born every day.'

I was puzzled by this last reference, for I had no recollection of Messer's having dealt with any assassin of the name he had mentioned. However I let it pass, for I was anxious to hear more of Raith's views on this subject.

'Is it the necessary qualities which are so rare in themselves,' I asked him eagerly, 'or is it not rather a consciousness of the use to which they ought to be put which is so generally wanting?'

'Both,' replied Raith with decision, eyeing me closely. 'The right combination of attributes will not often be found in one individual. He will be a man marked off from his fellows by superior mental powers, by rigid self-discipline, by knowledge and breadth of judgment, by the capacity for quick thought and decisive action. He will be able to view the largest events impersonally, objectively, and, if need be, coldly. But above all he must be a man of irreducible inner strength, pure and undeviating in the centre of his being, implacably devoted to the path which he has chosen to tread.'

A vivid flame soared up in my consciousness. It was myself of whom Raith was speaking. He had described me to the last hair! It could be no other! I blushed scarlet.

'But it is true also,' my mysterious double was continuing in his discourse, 'that rare though such a creature may be, many such a one may live out his life without ever coming to the realisation of where his true destiny lies. Such waste is terrible to contemplate, but it must often occur. For the right man to appear at the right moment and know what it is that he must do, an element must be present of what some might call chance or fate, and others attribute to a cosmic favour. But any of us may perhaps be instrumental in promoting such a possibility. That is why,' he finished with a rather unpleasant smile, 'I make it my business to recommend Dr. Messer's work to anyone who might be capable of entertaining even an inkling of its significance.'

My mind was in complete turmoil. I longed to tell my mentor of what was in my heart, but I dared not do so. Anyway, I was probably in too great a state of excitement to have articulated properly, but I attempted to do so.

'Well, I see you are ready to go home,' said Raith with a sardonic expression, contemplating me with something not unlike contempt, 'and I shall detain you no longer.'

Before I had time to answer he was gone, and such was my state of mind that I realised only half an hour after his departure that he had taken his leave without so much as asking for the copy of *Famous Assassins*, to collect which had presumably been the purpose of his visit. I had in fact left the book in my flat that morning, but to my amazement and no little distress and annoyance I discovered on going up there that it was gone! I had locked the place carefully on going down to the shop and there was no conceivable way in which anyone could have gained access without my knowledge. It was yet another provoking mystery in the series which had gathered around Raith and the wonderful book.

It was not long before I cared little about its disappearance, in fact, for its work was already done. The tormenting uncertainty of purpose, which had plagued me ever since my childhood discovery that I was unfitted for the career of musical composition on which I had set my heart, was now on the instant dissolved. Now my future was decided, and the task for which I felt myself to be supremely fitted offered itself seductively before me. The sense of my personal superiority, which had been part of my consciousness for so long but had often seemed ludicrously out of tune with the actualities of my life, now had a clear and coherent focus. I was set apart to improve the lot of mankind by acts of public and private assassination. Moreover, a potential victim lay immediately to hand: none other than Anthony Augustus, etc., Sykes-Buffington, 14th Viscount Gadarene. If *that* little deed could be accomplished, with what adoration would I be regarded by Jenny-lass! Wee Tam could say farewell to her for ever. Such grandiose and self-flattering thoughts pervaded my mind as I contemplated the career that lay ahead of me. I was in no hurry to begin, however: it was necessary first to accustom myself to the idea, to nurture and develop those special qualities which Raith had enumerated as necessary to the calling and which I had the rare good fortune to possess.

Three days after the second visit by Mr. Raith to Bookless and Bone's, President Kennedy was assassinated in Dallas, Texas. To me the event was a confirmatory sign that the day of my ministry was at hand.

IV

UNDER STRAIN

My mood during the months that followed was very strange. On the one hand I was elated by the exaltation which accompanied my new-found sense of mission, and eager to prepare myself for the action; on the other, I continued to be much more irked and wounded by Jenny's prolonged baulking of my amorous designs. I felt indeed that it was outrageous that she should thus persist in carelessly slighting so rare and irreplaceable a person as myself. She seemed totally unaware of her good fortune in attracting the attentions of one who was destined to such exceptional achievements, and I grew sullen and resentful as a result of my continued failure to make any further headway in this important concern of mine. The contrast between my revealed potential and the frustration of my present circumstances inflamed my pride in a way that began to make me drink far more than was good for me; and for much of the time, without being exactly inebriated, I was in a state of chronic alcoholic saturation.

This may partly have been the cause of the lurid and distasteful dreams with which I was increasingly troubled at this time. I can date their commencement, however, with some confidence from the visit of Mr. Raith and my acquaintance with the work of E.V. Messer. In many of these dreams I relived experiences of my waking life, but in a different hue and with fantastic and horrifying outcomes which seemed to reveal to me dark potentialities in my nature, tendencies towards brutality and sadism. The barrier between my conscious and unconscious worlds appeared, again, increasingly fragile, and I found myself indulging in behaviour which in heightened form was mirrored in the cruel fictions of my sleeping mind.

There was my treatment of Miss Crow, for instance. Miss Crow was a dear old lady who stayed in the neighbouring stair, and on occasions, if I met her coming in from shopping heavily laden with parcels, I would oblige her by carrying them up to her flat. She had for long been expressing a wish that I should drop in of an evening for a glass of sherry, and eventually I did so. As I sat by the fire in her sitting-room sipping my Bristol Cream I was unaccountably overtaken by an impulse to torment this delightful old person with my tongue.

'Giles would be my favourite nephew,' she was saying benignly, 'if I had favourites. Giles is the one who would look after me if I ever reached the stage where I couldn't look after myself. He's often told me that.'

'Would you not think of going into a home,' I was impelled treacherously to suggest, 'rather than be a burden to Giles? Many old people nowadays prefer not to be a burden to their relatives if they can possibly avoid it.'

Miss Crow looked crestfallen. 'I've thought of that, of course,' she said hastily. 'I've thought of it often. But Giles would insist, that's the trouble. "You will live with us, Auntie. No arguments, now!" That's the way he always puts it.'

'You have to bear in mind, I think,' said I, 'that Giles may really be counting on you to refuse just as insistently. After all, let's be realistic, who wants to be burdened with an arthritic old woman? It's not even as if you were his mother, he owes you nothing, you're only his aunt. He certainly wants you to refuse, Miss Crow. If he has made the offer, you see, made it insistently, then he is free to accept your refusal with a clear conscience. That's the way Giles is thinking. Of course, since he's made the offer, you are perfectly within your rights to accept. Giles's happiness needn't really concern you too much. You can say, "to hell with Giles," if you like, "he's offered and I'm accepting, so to hell with him". It all depends on whether you're able to live with your conscience.'

I was getting quite worked up, and took a big gulp of my sherry.

'I'd just be living in a converted bus at the bottom of the garden,' piped Miss Crow, pleadingly. 'Giles has said he can lay his hands on one quite cheaply.'

'A converted bus!' I leapt to my feet. 'A *converted bus*! Do you realise what you're saying, woman? Have you, I wonder, the remotest idea of what it would *cost* to convert a bus to the needs of a decrepit, decaying, arthritic old woman? Have you the least conception of what's involved? Oh, you've really got me going now. A converted bus, indeed!'

To underline my feelings about the matter, I emptied the remainder of my sherry down my throat and fairly banged the glass down on the occasional table, which caused Miss Crow to raise her hands to her mouth with a little shriek. At that, I'm afraid, I lost my head completely. Towering above her chair, I shouted at her incoherently.

'You disgust me, you old people!' I fairly bellowed. 'The arrogance, the crass self-centred impudence of you! Don't worry, Miss Crow, I'm not a violent man, I'm not going to hit you, much as you may deserve it. I would quite willingly pick you up like a rag doll and batter your head against that wall, it's true, but I won't, because I haven't the guts, that's what it boils down to, I suppose, I just haven't the guts!'

I think Miss Crow had fainted by this time, at any rate she had turned ashen grey, the sweat had broken out on her brow and her head was rolling about on her breast.

'Do you hear what I'm saying, woman?' I shouted in exasperation. 'Oh, what's the use, I might as well be talking to a tailor's dummy!'

I stormed out of the house and slammed the door behind me. By the time I reached my own flat I had more or less calmed down, and soon forgot the whole incident; however the next morning, just as I was about to go out, there came a timid ring at the door-bell and there stood Miss Crow, small and humble.

'I just wanted to apologise for last night,' she faltered.

'Don't say a thing,' I replied smiling, and dismissed her apology with a deprecating wave of the hand. 'I never thought twice about it. Consider the matter closed and forgotten.'

'But it was a dreadful thing to have said,' she protested feebly, 'to have thought of putting Giles to all that expense after all he's done for me...'

'As a matter of fact I think you were quite right,' I interrupted her, 'I'd say it's the least he could do for his old aunt, quite the least.'

'Oh, but the expense!' exclaimed Miss Crow. 'I must have been imagining it when I said "a converted bus", perhaps it was just an old bus.'

'*What?*' I said, raising my voice, 'Do you mean to say he'd let you live in an *un*converted bus? He sounds a right bastard to me, this Giles.'

'Oh, no!' cried Miss Crow anxiously, shaking her head. 'Giles is the kindest soul!'

'Kind? Did I hear you aright? *Kind?*' I exploded. 'He makes a crippled, dying old woman live in a run-down ramshackle old bus and you call him *kind*? You must be going out of your mind! By God I know how I'd deal with Giles if I ever ran across him!'

At this point the terror and consternation on Miss Crow's face were such that I though better of my outburst and began to back-track a little, endeavouring to soothe the old lady's shattered nerves and to give the impression that I had been carried away by well-intended indignation on her behalf; so that although Miss Crow was now clearly very unsure of me we parted on reasonably civilised terms. But that night I relived the scene in dream, and there, far from exhibiting any such symptoms of a better nature, I followed up my verbal assault by shaking Miss Crow as a dog might a rat, until she howled like a trapped beast, when I threw her roughly against the wall.

'Don't take that personally,' I said as she tottered and panted, 'I was merely indicating the kind of reception your dutiful nephew would receive if he ever darkened my doorstep.'

'Oh, you're a hateful, wicked man!' gasped the spirited Miss Crow of my dream.

At that I gave her a back-hander across the face and she dropped to her knees; then before she had a chance to retaliate I went in with the boot. With the unnatural clarity of dream I half-heard, half-felt the faint crunch of splintering bone as her nose collapsed against my toe. Her head went back, a bloodied mask of horror. She fell over against the wall then tried to rise, shielding her face with one arm. Thud! My boot was in her gut...

I awoke, quivering with an ecstasy which soon dissolved into a sickening sense of shame as I contemplated the extent of the depravity which prevailed in my unconscious. I began to wonder whether I could be under some maleficent influence; but reflecting that hardness of heart was a necessary attribute for a political assassin, did my best to still the troubled movements of my conscience with the thoughts that the powers that be were shaping me for the tasks that lay ahead.

In spite of these attempts at self-reassurance I found myself at this time repeatedly tormented by the fear of incipient madness, and on the pretence of worry about my compulsive drinking habits managed to persuade my doctor to refer me to a psychiatrist for guidance. On the appointed day I presented myself at a warren of medical consulting-rooms in a crescent in the New Town. I was shown into the waiting-room by a receptionist, and there I found an insinuating, mousy little man who asked me in a Newcastle accent whether I was waiting to see Dr. Fenelon, the psychiatrist.

'Yes,' I replied coldly.

'Do you mind if I go first?' he asked ingratiatingly, 'I've been having terrible nervous troubles. You don't mind, do you?' he suggested with a fawning look in his eye, coming up to me and making as if to lay his hand on my arm.

'No,' I said shortly, recoiling with grim distaste.

He fell back, muttering, and resumed his seat, but kept glancing over at me furtively and resentfully, and mouthing inaudible remarks which appeared to be directed against myself.

'No, I don't mind if you go first,' I added disdainfully after a while, 'but I think you ought to know that Dr. Fenelon is not a psychiatrist, though most GP's refer to him under that euphemism so as not to cause their patients useless alarm. In fact he is a brain surgeon, specialising in frontal lobotomies.'

That shut him up. He sat there with his effeminate little hands outstretched on his thighs, looking at his knees, quaking visibly and sweating copiously, until his name was called. I was left alone in the waiting-room and, when about half an hour had elapsed without anything further happening, I was overcome by a sudden access of pride and resentment. With whom did Dr. Fenelon think he was dealing? Was I to be kept waiting indefinitely at the pleasure of some arrogant, insentient shrink? I would give him something to think about. I found the receptionist's office.

'My appointment was for three,' I stated icily, 'and it is now 3.35. Kindly inform Dr. Fenelon of my departure.' Without awaiting a reply I took my leave.

When I dreamt of this unremarkable and indecisive incident the facts became subject to the most outrageous and absurd ramifications. The dream depicted me kneeling outside the door of Dr. Fenelon's consulting-room, with my ear at the keyhole, deceitfully intruding upon the secrets of the mousy little patient's psyche.

'You have to remember, I think,' the psychiatrist was saying, 'that great variations are possible within the range of normality.' But even greater ones are possible within the range of abnormality, I thought to myself.

'But let me tell you this, doctor,' came the mousy little Geordie's eager voice, and I strained my ears to hear every syllable as he launched into a catalogue of pitiable obsessions and inadequacies which it warmed my heart to hear. There's always someone worse off than yourself, I thought: but as if to disprove this judgment the door was unexpectedly thrown open, and the psychiatrist, a gigantic Frenchman with one leg, towered above me as I crouched guiltily in the shadows.

'*Espece de cochon!*' he shouted furiously, and took a swipe at me with his crutch. Behind him I caught a glimpse of the wretched little patient crowing delightedly over my discomfiture. Turning to flee, I next behold the receptionist standing open-mouthed before me, an expression of horror and outrage gathering slowly on her countenance. Utterly shamed and discredited, I slithered past her and charged out into the street, pursued by the vengeful Dr. Fenelon. I ran and ran, but always behind me I thought I heard the rhythmic crash of the psychiatrist's crutches on the flagstones and his strong, irate cries. I crossed Princes Street, and following the No. 9 bus route did not cease in my headlong rush until I reached the west end of Colinton Road, a distance of some four miles. There my dream took me down Paties Road, heading for Colinton Dell, where at last I began to feel safe from the clutches of Dr. Fenelon and confident that I had shaken him off. At the entrance to the Dell I met an elderly gentleman with a worried look on his face.

'I don't advise you to go into the Dell, sir,' he said, trembling, 'there's a madman at large down there.'

'That is not surprising,' I replied, 'for it is there that all the madmen of Scotland are wont to foregather of a summer's evening, to contend for beds among the branches of thorn trees and to eat delightful watercress. At such times, indeed, Colinton Dell can boast one of the finest ranges of lunatics and simpletons in these islands.'

The old gentleman hurried away on hearing this news, but I went on boldly into the Dell, and before long found myself in the midst of a veritable assembly of mentally disturbed persons. These could be divided into two principal categories: those who progressed very slowly with very small steps, kept their arms straight by their sides and stared at the ground undeviatingly as they walked; and those who covered the ground exuberantly with immense strides, swung their arms frenetically and grinned all the time. But one madman in particular caught my fancy. He was a low-slung, bow-legged maniac with a cowboy gait, strong in the upper limbs, crop-headed, beetle-browed, cross-eyed, wrinkled-nosed. As he proceeded along the pathway he mouthed away to himself incessantly, shouted incomprehensibly, sometimes singing a snatch of some popular ditty, though with little taste. Every now and again he would unexpectedly spring sideways or backwards, fists at the ready, as if to face some assailant about to leap on him from the undergrowth. When he was quite near me he sprang up onto the parapet above the Water of Leith and shambled along it with the clumsy sure-footedness of an ape. He seemed to be living in a little world of his own. I had begun to think that we would pass each other without incident when he jumped down and stood gibbering gracelessly before me.

'What has driven you out of your wits?' I asked kindly. He made an incoherent grunting noise, slobbering at the mouth.

'Do not be afraid to answer me,' I pursued, 'for I myself am out of my mind.'

'Then we are two of a kind,' he replied. 'Always of weak intellect and stunted physique, I was during my childhood constantly battered about the head and grievously chastised by my hard-drinking stepfather for my many misdemeanours, and on two occasions thrown headlong down a stair. This it was that reduced me to the pitiful state in which you now behold me. And yourself? What misfortune may it be, unhappy man, that has caused you and your senses to part company?'

'Unrequited love,' I replied. So we chatted amicably enough for some minutes about our respective lunacies, the other often emitting raucous shouts and leaping about unpredictably. Then, quite unexpectedly, a very disturbing thing began to happen. The madman's face, which up till now had seemed, if not positively sympathetic, at any rate not unfriendly, became diffused for me with a quality of inexpressible menace. It was not that he himself had altered his expression, but that I had come to perceive in it a property of which I had previously been unaware, and which I was not at once able to identify. He was not sneering, yet his features seemed to *express* a sneer, and in that expression there was something hellishly familiar. I groaned in my sleep as I strove, as if my life depended upon it, to bring that familiarity to the pitch of memory ... It was the wrinkled-nosed laundryman. The laundryman, tormenting spectre of my childhood! I was instantly awake.

It was in the wake of this grotesque dream that a peculiar unease began to insinuate itself into my mind, an unease which I endeavoured constantly to thrust back into the shadows before it was able to take on the embodiment of thought. This unease consisted of an association, almost but not quite an identity in my mind between the wrinkled-nosed laundryman and the sinister Mr. Raith. Such an identity could scarcely be accounted for on rational grounds—there was no resemblance of feature between the two, if anything only a fleeting sugges-tion in the way the mouth moved, the way the eyes shifted ... it must be entirely subjective. Yet the suggestion seemed to lie more rootedly than in any facial analogy, and it was because it arose spontaneously from the deeps of my own consciousness that I resisted it so stubbornly. I could not but resist it, for the laundryman had always been the embodiment to me of all that was threatening, hostile and unknown, while Mr. Raith on the contrary had been the agent of my regeneration, the one who had brought my destiny to clarity and coherence before my eyes ... It could be nothing but an illusion, the evil fruit of brooding and inaction.

I determined therefore to disperse with the wind of action the noxious vapours that were poisoning my mind. My disturbances were the necessary accompaniment of procrastination and avoidance of my duty. It was now necessary, if I was not to become one of those sad and lost figures who, through some final failure of nerve, never accomplish the work for which alone they are intended, that I turn aspiration into achievement. I began accordingly to lay my plans for the assassination of the 14th Viscount Gadarene.

V

I PREPARE FOR MY MISSION

In practical terms the task which I had set myself did not seem to be over-exacting. I quickly devised a rough and ready plan for getting myself to Teuchtershards, which I sometimes felt was rather slipshod but which nevertheless did not seem to have any obvious flaws or disadvantages. For some time the Viscount's Highland factor had been sending small consignments of eighteenth-century books from the library there to Bookless and Bone's; apparently it was felt that the sums they might realise would outweigh any cultural loss which the estate would sustain as a result of their disposal. Many of the books were of genuine value and interest, and I determined to write purporting to be a partner in the business, expressing a great desire to inspect the library, and offering to value it and advise as to its possible classification or dispersal. If I received a favourable response I would name a period safely within the grouse-shooting season as convenient for my visit, and then insinuate myself into a position where I might have an opportunity of getting close to Viscount Gadarene, if not actually making his acquaintance.

At first I toyed with the idea of proposing this expedition to Uncle Sean and thus going to Teuchtershards with complete and genuine credentials, but I decided that the risk was too great that my uncle would either pour cold water on the scheme or, more likely, take it up and then announce his intention of going himself or sending wee Tam instead of me, no doubt using my inexperience as a convenient excuse for an act of sheer spite. I had a fortnight's holiday due to me and it would be much safer to say nothing to my uncle and to make use of this time for the enactment of my first great deed. I wrote to the factor accordingly, and after about three weeks, to my great surprise and gratification, received a most charming letter from Viscount Gadarene himself, written from his London address, expressing marked enthusiasm for my proposal. While not being exactly a bookworm himself, as he confessed with endearing frankness, he had always had a great affection and respect for the old volumes bequeathed him by his forefathers, and had long harboured an inclination to have the collection expertly assessed. He suggested that if I were to make the journey to Teuchtershards so as to coincide with a few days in September which fell between two shooting parties, I would be assured of a warm welcome and be the recipient of some traditional Highland hospitality.

For some time after hearing this news I felt truly as if I were walking on air, and I was convinced that my intentions must have earned the approval of Heaven. I had not yet ventured to think beyond the point of establishing myself at Teuchtershards, and had given no consideration to the question of how I was actually to do away with Viscount Gadarene, whether I would shoot, stab or poison, drown, strangle or suffocate him. Too much seemed to depend on a variety of contingencies which might come into play once I was on the spot and knew the lie of the land. Indeed I was rather loth to envisage too minutely the various methods of dispatch which might lie open to me. There was time enough for all that, I told myself, and I had a large contempt for mere matters of detail. I preferred to dwell, with a warm glow gladdening me within, upon the immense psychological release which I knew I would experience when the heroic act had been effected and I had created myself anew as one of the chosen band celebrated by E.V. Messer. Even in anticipation a measure of pleasant, tired spiritual satiety pervaded my senses at these thoughts.

As the time of my historic expedition grew nearer, however, my mood underwent a subtle change. Not to put too fine a point upon it, I suffered a slight attack of cold feet. My enthusiasm for the ideas of Messer had always been directed towards their metaphysical implications rather than to the practicalities involved; and I was more attracted to the spiritual distinction which would accrue to the lofty soul which dared to take upon itself this high destiny, than to the concomitant necessity for butchery. I realised well enough that I would have to think seriously about this latter consideration, but as soon as I attempted to do so I found my mind always drifting away towards loftier horizons, and I was honest enough to admit to myself that I had failed totally to overcome certain inhibitions regarding the taking of human life which had been instilled into me by my upbringing.

One Sunday morning I was walking on the woodland path that runs by the Firth of Forth through the Dalmeny estate, and pondering these matters in my mind. It was a fine fresh summer's day with a light breeze blowing, the birds were singing, and through the trees I could see the clear blue of the firth beyond the beach. But I walked mostly with my eyes cast down towards the ground, sunk in morose thoughts. As I was passing on my left the open, grassy promontory which stands above Hound Point, I became aware of a figure approaching from that direction to join the path. Looking up, I was astonished to find that it was none other than Raith, whom I had not seen for many months and had not really expected to encounter again.

'Do you come here often?' I asked him satirically as he came up to me. I was greatly taken aback by his sudden appearance and found myself adopting a bantering tone to mask my confusion.

'Whistle and I'll come to you, my lad,' he replied with a nasty smile. I had no idea what to say next, and we walked along for a few minutes in silence. I felt acutely uncomfortable, as if I had been surprised in some illicit act. I was aware as I walked of Raith constantly glancing at me, as if challenging me to initiate some conversation, and I began to feel hightly resentful.

'This Dr. Messer of yours,' I blurted out angrily at last, 'he doesn't seem to have much to say about the morality of what he recommends.' I felt rather ashamed as soon as I had spoken, and imagined that Raith would conclude that I was merely using morality as an escape-route to secure a retreat from my resolution. For some reason it never crossed my mind that Raith should be ignorant of my intentions.

He raised his eyebrows. 'I should have thought that he was concerned wholly with morality,' he said at once. 'A higher morality than that on which you have been reared, of course. Not the cursed Christian morality, which assumes that there is no other life in the universe than that of man. You are something of a musician, are you not?' he added with a malicious intonation. I was too hurt to reply. 'Music, now,' he continued, 'is an expression of a life which is greater and profounder than the life of man, though man participates in that greater life.'

He stopped suddenly in his walk, and grabbing me by the shoulders swept his other arm along the vista of the beach with a grand gesture.

'Look at that beach,' he said, 'inconceivably older than the whole history of man! What does that beach know of morality? What does morality have to do with the immeasurably intricate order of its beauty? Yet man can destroy that order in the tiniest instant—and will. Look at that age-old beach and then think of all the misery and ugliness to which man has attained during his minute span. How do the two compare? Can you assert that man deserves to survive?'

'I am a man myself,' I protested. 'If the human race goes down, I go down with it.'

'So do we all,' replied Raith with a cold, hollow laugh. 'It boots not. If man fails, God will sweep him away. He'll sweep man away if man fails, and express Himself in some better form.'

'Do you believe in God, then?' I asked with astonishment.

'Of course. It is no longer possible to doubt the existence of God, that will soon be clear. The only remaining questions relate to His nature. Such a belief is not faith, but certainty.' He laughed again, his face as bleak as winter. 'To believe steadfastly that life has no meaning—*that* is how to keep oneself upright on the crutches of faith. Such will be our comfort and

125

assurance—but how many will be strong enough to understand that?'

I did not fully understand what he was saying, but something in his tone and manner made the hairs on the back of my neck rise, and the blood coursed violently through my veins. The strange man was speaking coldly but with an inhuman exaltation, and I felt for him a fascinated repulsion. I was at once thrilled and terrified by his insight into the need to transcend the very idea of man; yet I felt a curious reluctance to accede to his dogmatic assertions without offering at least a token show of resistance.

'Intellectually I might go along with you,' I ventured, 'but emotionally I find it difficult.'

To my dismay he rounded on me furiously, his eyes flashing with savage scorn. 'The foul quagmire which the human race is making out of the natural world is the direct responsibility of people like you,' he cried, 'who retain the abominable illusion that man is the centre of the universe. He is not. The natural world is much stronger than man and will destroy him if he seeks to destroy it. The apocalypse will be a purely human one, you can bank on that—and it will be the result of the hateful world-view of the Christians, which sets man at the centre of Creation by identifying the fate of the universe with his fate. But when I say that man will be swept away I mean that *man* will be swept away. I don't mean that the universe will be swept away on man's account.'

An instinct in me seemed to assent to this grim analysis, yet my spirit shrank from adapting itself to so fierce a perspective.

'So you believe in some impersonal hope from beyond the fate of mankind?' I asked Raith uncertainly.

We had started walking again, but now he stopped, and stood across my path. His eyes were shining with a sort of impersonal fanaticism, and seemed to express no human emotion, but a final timeless callousness.

'Look,' said Raith, 'this is how it is. Eternal life continues in spite of all destruction, as we know in our entrails. That is why, in tragedy, we assent to the destruction of the hero, who is the symbolic figure of humankind. In just the same way we must assent in God's tragedy to the destruction of humankind itself: for it, too, is nothing but a phenomenon, and its removal has not the least effect on the life beyond appearance.'

He ceased, and I stood in silence before him, quite numbed by the intensity of this discourse. His fanatical expression gradually fell away from him, and he began to resume the detached, ironical and scornful look which was more habitual with him. We were now standing before the great park surrounding Dalmeny House, and suddenly he made a gesture towards the vast and stately building.

'This scene of opulence reminds me,' he said quietly, as he fixed me steadily with his eyes, 'to wish you luck at Teuchtershards.' And with that, and even before I had time to be dumbfounded, he turned on his heel and strode off very fast in the direction of the Almond ferry, and soon was lost to sight among the trees.

Though its relevance to my mission was really only very indirect, this latest conversation with my mysterious acquaintance had the immediate effect of strengthening my previously somewhat flagging resolve, and of dispersing the reservations and scruples which I had half-consciously begun to entertain with regard to the coming assassination. The thought that I might be too weak a person in my moral nature to embrace the grim but exhilarating philosophy which Raith had expounded, that I could possibly have been mistaken in supposing myself one of the exceptional iron-clad souls of whom Messer had written with such eloquence, was now too painful for me even to contemplate, and I thrust such suspicions from me with derision. To have done otherwise, indeed, would have been to undermine the assumption upon which the entire conduct of my life was now founded.

One day shortly before my holiday was due to begin, my Uncle Sean called me, not for the first time, into his little nest at the back of the bookshop. He was wearing a   for some reason, and looking tired and sad as he contemplated me from above his steel-framed spectacles. Even in the height of summer he looked pinched with cold and blue about the mouth. Our little war had reached a condition of stalemate, and for some months we had been observing a mistrustful truce.

'Where are you going for your holiday?' he asked me expressionlessly, as if it were a great ordeal for him to be obliged to make conversation. I considered advising him to mind his own business, but thought better of it.

'To the west coast,' I replied, and determined to volunteer nothing further.

'Would you consider leaving us an address where you can be reached?' he asked in the same tone as before, looking past me in an affected manner at a picture on the wall.

'I would not,' I said, 'my holidays are my own affair.'

'And I have little interest in your whereabouts, believe me,' he responded with too great an alacrity, as if he had been anticipating and even hoping for such a reply, 'it is simply that your father is poorly, that is all. He has been poorly in fact for quite some time now, but I felt that it would be a waste of time my mentioning the fact in view of your marked deficiency in filial piety.' He was unable to maintain his air of drooping indifference throughout this speech, and finished on a note of glib smugness, his colour even rising just perceptibly through the power of his own oratory. I of course made absolutely no rejoinder to his leading remarks, so as not to give him the satisfaction of knowing whether they might have touched, shamed, offended or riled me. I looked at him coolly but respectfully, waiting for him to resume. I felt immeasurably superior to him in every way.

'Have you no conscience whatsoever, then?' he smirked, putting his head to one side so that the tassel of his fez flapped about ludicrously, and placing his hands on his hips in an almost obscene, flaunting gesture.

'I have,' I said, and waited once more. I really had him on toast, now. He had called this interview, and I had not failed to answer any of his questions. He had already imparted essentially all the factual information which he had to offer, and it was up to me what I did with it. For all he knew I might now act with exemplary filial piety, perhaps devote my holiday in its entirety to ministering to my father on his sick bed and yet say nothing to Uncle Sean of my intentions at this point in time. There was nothing he could charge me with; indeed he was on remarkably thin ice, for I could with a large measure of justice have turned on him and upbraided him soundly for having kept my father's condition from me thus far. He was desperate to elicit some kind of response from me, which would have given him further room to manoeuvre and perhaps to place me at a disadvantage; but if he persisted too stubbornly in his efforts he might end up by making a complete fool of himself, and risk behaving as if he were haranguing a brick wall. He was no doubt dimly and incoherently aware of all this, so he had no recourse but to send me packing in an implicit admission of defeat.

'Oh, get out, get out!' he exclaimed petulantly and flapped his hands like a goose trying to take off from water. 'You make me very angry sometimes,' he added, in a particularly weak attempt to save a measure of face; and I retired without uttering another syllable, leaving him with the dubious pleasure of having had the last word.

It did occur to me that I might make some further enquiries as to the seriousness of my father's illness, but my pride prevented me from doing so. He had kicked me out, after all, and if he wanted me back he could ask for me. I did not know whether Uncle Sean had been acting on his own initiative in instigating the sordid little scene that I have described, but I felt that if any approaches to me were to have reasonable hopes of success they must be seen to be thoroughly open and above board. My uncle's underhand tactics were the last thing that could be expected to influence me favourably in such a matter. Besides, when all was said and done I had enough to think about at the moment. In less than a week I would be at Teuchtershards.

I seemed to see my friends and companions now as from a great height; they appeared as ephemeral, puppet-like creatures who belonged to a world of child-like innocence to which my high destiny must make me for ever a stranger. I could now look even on Jenny-lass as one who had once played a minor part in the life of the man who was about to assassinate the 14th Viscount Gadarene. Such thoughts were in my mind as I took my leave of her and wee Tam outside a pub on the night before I was due to depart. After we had said our farewells and set off on our separate ways I heard a shout behind me and turned to see Tam hurrying back eagerly to tell me something he had forgotten.

'Did you hear about this Yankee cavalry officer that was going into action against the Comanches?' he enquired breathlessly.

'No,' I rejoined with weary good nature.

'He raises his sword above his head and shouts tae the troops: "Let battle comanch!"'

Tam snorted triumphantly as he delivered the punchline. I stood and watched him as he charged off to catch up with Jenny, waving his hands above his head and crying repeatedly, 'Let battle comanch! Let battle comanch!'; and reflected wistfully as I watched that the distance between us could be measured only in light years.

VI

THE JOURNEY

I set out on my fateful journey on a mild, overcast, drizzling afternoon, travelling by train to Glasgow. I had promised my uncle that I would undertake a small item of business there on behalf of the shop, so although there was otherwise no necessity to travel by that route I was obliged to spend my first night there. Being rather short of money I booked into the YMCA, then spent a gloomy evening drinking by myself. By this time I was longing for action, and the enforced delay made me extremely jumpy and nervous. As a result I drank a good deal more that evening than was sensible.

By the time I got back to the hostel it was eleven o'clock and an old porter was in the act of locking the inmates in for the night. It was only with difficulty that I prevailed upon this irascible old fellow to permit my entry. He had his shirt sleeves rolled up and a disreputable, food-stained waistcoat hanging open to reveal a revolting corporation, and kept up an intermittent barrage of mutterings and curses until all formalities had been completed. I think he had been drinking. As I made my way up to the desk with my canvas bag in my hand I had to suffer the inscrutable gaze of a number of Arabs and Persians who were sitting on plastic-covered benches in the lobby, eating chips out of paper pokes. A disgusting atmosphere of antiseptic and stale cooking pervaded the place, and the walls were thick with cyclostyled notices prohibiting this and that. When I had signed in and received my key, the porter took me up a couple of flights in the lift, indicated a room with an ill-tempered grunt, and left me to it.

I found myself in an overheated cell, bare but for bed, table, wardrobe, basin and prohibitory notices. It was two or three hours before my normal bedtime, and I had neglected to bring any reading matter with me. To my great distress, moreover, The Gideons had failed to provide this place with a supply of buckshee Bibles, probably because of the paucity of even nominal Christians among the guests of the YMCA. The window looked out onto a flat roof which even in the dark I could see was littered with broken bottles. I paced about gloomily up and down the cell for some time, often knocking against the meagre furniture in my semi-inebriated condition, trying to put off for as long as possible the necessity to get undressed. It would be a very long night, and I knew that I would shortly be assailed by hunger pangs. Eventually I came to the sensible conclusion that the best hope of fending these off lay in trying to get to sleep as soon as possible.

I had not long been in bed before a record player not far down the corridor began to play some very monotonous oriental music, and so it continued to do for the best part of an hour. At one point I got up to scour the notice-board for regulations outlawing the playing of music during the night, but to my surprise and chagrin found nothing. Almost every other pastime, innocent or otherwise, that the mind of man could devise was prohibited, but not that. Eventually this noise ceased, and after much tossing and turning and one episode of sleep paralysis I managed to doze off. Almost immediately, it seemed, I was awakened by a transistor radio belting out popular music from the direction of the washroom, and soon it was joined by several others, all receiving different stations. Young men now began to shout at each other, seemingly over great distances, in Arabic and Turkish. The time was a quarter to three; I was hot and sweaty, exhausted and very hungry.

When this confusion of Babel had continued for some time, not to be outdone I got up and flung the door of my room open, and emerging into the corridor bellowed in the direction of the ablutions, in tones of demonic fury, a number of impressive

phrases in indifferent Gaelic. *'Sin agad bodach ruadh!'* I shouted
tempestuously, which being interpreted is, 'That is a codling!'
(literally, 'There at you a reddish old man!'); and again, *'tha
ball aig na gillean ach chan eil ball aig na caileagan,'* which being
interpreted is, 'the boys have a ball but the girls haven't a ball.'
These quite irrelevant utterances, surprisingly, were not without
their effect, for a stillness as of death suddenly descended upon
the washing area, and was even maintained for quite a decent
spell. Presumably there was but little Gaelic at those people.
Little by little, however, shouts began to erupt afresh, transistors
were turned up, the decibels started to rise again, and before
long the oriental hubbub had attained unprecedented levels of
intensity. There was little I could do but curl up into a ball
under the bedclothes and wait for this visitation to cease.

Gradually, very gradually, the noise began to level out and
then to abate; but only after many unfounded hopes had been
raised and dashed did the last cry die away and silence descend
upon that troubled hostelry. Dawn had broken and Phoebus'
golden car was due to pop over the horizon at any moment
when I sank into a troubled sleep, and began to dream a very
bad dream indeed—nightmare would not be too strong a term
for it. I can attribute its horror only to the confused and lurid
impressions of the preceding hours. I dreamt that the wrinkle-
nosed laundryman was after me. I was in a place that had always
terrified me as a child, the pathway to our neighbour's garden,
which was reached through a very narrow gate in a high stone
wall, and thickly surrounded on both sides by dusty holly bushes.
Whenever I had occasion to go up that path I had always stared
rigidly in front of me, terrified to glance for even an instant to
either side, for I was convinced that nothing less than the Ultimate
Horror lurked among those bushes. I was standing there now,
and against my will something compelled me to look to my
right. There, crouching between a holly bush and the high wall
like a cat about to spring, was the wrinkle-nosed laundryman. I
turned and fled, and by one of those kaleidoscopic shifts familiar
to all who dream, he was now pursuing me along the rooftops

of a row of terraced houses on the other side of the road. He was so close on my heels that I could feel his noxious breath on the back of my neck; and coming to the end of the row I turned at bay against a chimney-stack. Facing my enemy I saw that his features, horribly distorted by a demonic grin, were now unmistakably those of the enigmatic Mr. Raith. Fixing me with a scornful and glittering eye, he slowly drew from within the folds of his black coat a scouting-knife which I possessed as a child, and began to unsheath it. I leapt frantically down the sloping roof, plunged off the edge and awoke screaming for all I know in colloquial Arabic. I may say that I was most appreciably shaken by this highly significant dream.

That night's fitful slumbers were finally ended for me at seven o'clock when the occupant of the room next to mine commenced chanting or wailing, what I took to be a prayer; this lasted for twenty-five minutes. No doubt it was a Moslem that was in him. My hunger would allow me no further rest, and I dressed and went downstairs to break my fast upon a fried egg swimming in grease, a rasher of cold and gristly bacon, two slices of leathery toast and a mug of execrably strong tea. Thus fortified I set forth upon the next stage of my journey.

I felt more like a pilgrim than an ordinary traveller. I was a consecrated mission upon which I had set out and my destination might some day acquire the character of a shrine to which future generations would journey with reverence to make their obeisances to the symbolic birthplace of a noble idea. Such thoughts cheered my spirits a little and gave me strength as I trudged that morning along the road out of Glasgow in an incontinent downpour, describing fruitless circles in the air with my right thumb as cars and lorries whizzed constantly and pitilessly past me, showering me frequently from top to toe, as if to ignore my pleas for a lift were an insufficient expression of their contemptuous spite.

At last fortune smiled upon me in the shape of a bland Englishman in a Jaguar. He had recently taken over the west of Scotland for his company, and that day he was making for

Oban. He told me that he often picked up hitch-hikers; he did a great deal of travelling, and being a gregarious type found that he missed having company if he was alone during the long hours on the road. It soon became apparent that what he missed was not so much company as an audience. A passenger like myself was no more than an excuse for him to hear the sound of his own voice. He was not at all interested in conversation and required only token grunts as a punctuated response to his twanging monologue. Indeed he seemed positively to resent any attempt on my part to contribute to the proceedings, and would simply override my tentative mutterings with his flat, insentient bray. The worst of all was that I was completely at his mercy, as we both understood very well. He was doing me a favour, and the price I had to pay was to suffer him gladly. He could take me a considerable proportion of my journey, the rain was still coming down as if it might never stop, and he could turf me out onto the road any moment he chose if I displeased him or failed to serve his purpose. Moreover he probably would. He was the type of arrogant, fatuously complacent individual who will not brook disagreement and who luxuriates in a position of power, however petty. So I was obliged to suffer humbly and even gratefully the deluge of his impertinent nonsense.

When we stopped at a pub for some sandwiches he began to hold forth on the subject of a 'humorous article' which he had been asked to write for the company magazine on the subject of his first year in Scotland. For some reason it was necessary to the satisfactory completion of this literary exercise that he should quote from 'Scots Wha Hae', and he began to question me in a loud voice about its meaning, to my great embarrassment, for several people were staring at us.

'Wot does all that gibberish mean, then?' he demanded with cocky but winning assurance.

'"Scots Wha Hae" means "Scots who have"', I explained ingratiatingly and as quickly as I could. '"Wha" just means "who" and "hae" means "have". An apostrophe may be inserted to indicate that the "v" has been left out,' I added with unctuous servility. A hundred miles in comfort on a wet day was what the approbation of this idiot was worth to me.

'Ow, I see, Scots wah high,' said the executive, nodding sagely. A murderous impulse seized me and shook my frame. My fists clenched convulsively in my lap, and for an instant it seemed that my career of outrage would have a premature commencement. But a moment later the man said something which almost made me pity him, for it revealed him, in all his well-covered affluence, to be most abjectly a slave. He was relating how in the past year he had rather come to enjoy living in Scotland.

'I must admit,' he said with disarming cheek, 'that when we first heard we were going to be moved up here we weren't exactly delirious at the prospect.'

I looked at him with my mouth open. The man regarded himself with equanimity as a chattel, who could be 'moved' hither and thither at whim by a superior will without reference to his wishes or desires. Of course it had now turned out that far from merely resigning himself to life in the wilds he was actually having a great time, but that was scarcely the point. He and his family had had no desire to come in the first place, but, slaves to the materialism and ambition which give to impersonal economic forces their powers of control, they had come unquestioningly. The man apparently saw nothing demeaning in such a condition and even seemed to experience it as natural and quite in the order of things. It was quite a little eye-opener to me, that. Yes, I learned something on that wet car journey from that deplorable man, even if indirectly, and I am not too proud to admit it.

By the time our roads diverged the rain had begun to slacken off, and I was not sorry when I had to walk for a few miles, on a fine road skirting a sea loch, before securing another lift. I felt glad to be free of the constricting and overbearing atmosphere of the Jaguar, and as I strode out filling my lungs with good sea air my spirits rose and my confidence expanded, and I sang my favourite hymns aloud to myself to keep my heart lifted up. 'Guide me, O thou great Jehovah,' I remember I sang that

afternoon, and 'To be a Pilgrim'. In due course I was picked
up by a beer lorry which took me all the way into Brieston, the
little fishing town from which the steamer was due to leave for
the island of my destination early the following morning.

I signed into the local hotel, had a long hot bath and ate a
hearty meal; then I went out for a walk in the cool September
air just as the light was beginning to fade. I walked for perhaps
a mile along the shore-road which led out of the village towards
a bleak point, beyond the harbour's mouth, which commanded
a view over the habitually gale-swept loch. A wind was getting
up now, indeed, and I felt some qualms of trepidation about
the prospects for tomorrow's voyage. When I reached the end
of the road, where it petered out upon the rocky promontory,
I was disagreeably struck by a tall, narrow house, grim and
grey-harled, which clung stubbornly to a mere patch of ground
between the rocks and gravel at the beach and the encroaching
buttress of the hills behind. There was something imposing yet
sinister about this storm-bleached place, and I stood gazing
reflectively at it for some time, lost in dismal thoughts. There
was no sign of human life about it, but it seemed pervaded by
ghostly presences, and I brooded upon it with morbid fascination,
feeling certain that some grim tale must attach to it. Dragging
myself away with a shudder at last I hurried back to the hotel
through the gathering gloom, and hastened to revive myself in
the warmth and animation of the public bar.

My mood was despondent again and it was not easy for me to
recover my spirits. I sat alone, surrounded by a throng of shouting
and laughing fishermen, removed by my special destiny from
human companionship, unpleasantly aware how fast the hour was
now approaching when my onerous and unenviable task would
have to be faced. Was I strong enough for it? That was what
tormented me. Most of the time I knew that I was; doubt was
a phantom only of these low moments, when my resources were
at their furthest ebb, when some trivial circumstance, perhaps,
interfered with the temperature of my emotional life. Tonight it
was doubtless the lugubrious influence of that ghostlike house,

which, acting on nerves jaded by a taxing journey following on a sleepless night, had thus disturbed my equilibrium and plunged me into introspective brooding. In an effort to boost my morale I began to add a malt whisky to every pint I consumed.

There was a group of fishermen drinking at a table not far from me, and one of them, taking no part in the conversation of his mates, was poring over a copy of the *Daily Express*. Something caught my eye and attracted my interest in the banner headline on the front page, but because of the way the man was holding the paper I was able to read only a tantalising couple of words, of ambiguous purport. I strove to reach a position where I could read the rest, but twist and turn as I might I could not do so; and the man was taking an inordinate time to read every page. Whenever he did finally get to the end of one, moreover, he would turn over the page very quickly in a great noisy flurry of paper before I had a chance to make out those words, and would then resume his previous attitude, or one which was equally unhelpful. Although he had never so much as glanced in my direction and I could not even see his face properly, in my depressed condition I became convinced that he knew quite well that I was trying to make out the headline, and that he was taking a perverse delight in preventing me from doing so, out of sheer spite. My hackles began to rise, and with every page that was eventually turned over with the same lack of benefit to myself, my indignation mounted uncontrollably. Finally he reached the back page, closed the paper and laid it flat on the table before him, immersing himself in the sports news with what I suspected to be a smirk upon what little I could see of his face. It was too much. I determined to confront and challenge him, and rose rather unsteadily to my feet. Even as I did so, the man himself stood up quite without warning and looked me full in the face. It was the wrinkle-nosed laundryman. I believe that my heart stopped beating for several seconds. I stood there gazing at him, and felt a cold sweat break out all over my body. A great buzzing sound arose in my ears, the room lurched before my eyes, and a woolliness as of cotton-wool obliterated all my faculties. I was about to faint. I turned and groped my way out of the bar and into the hall of the hotel, and managed somehow to stumble up the stairs and into my bedroom. With fumbling fingers I bolted the door and collapsed palpitating on the bed. I was certain that the laundryman had not been far behind me, and for an hour or two after that I believed that I heard him padding up and down in the corridor outside my room. For the second night running I slept less than soundly.

I was again afflicted with the nightmare of the previous day, nor indeed was I destined to be free of it for many nights to come. This time it was clear to me that the laundryman's commission was to bring me to justice for failure in my high purpose, and that this dream constituted a terrible warning. It was not an encouraging message to receive on the very eve of my arrival at Teuchtershards. As before, it was dawn when I dropped into an exhausted slumber. I had arranged on my arrival to be called early so as to give me plenty of time to catch the steamer; and when I was awakened at half-past-six by the chambermaid hammering on my door, I believed that it was Raith beating out on my skull, in a cryptic language which I could not translate, the meaning of my life and the pronouncement of my doom. I dressed hurriedly in the morning chill, bolted some breakfast, and shivering from debility and a slight fever boarded the steamer five minutes before it was due to sail.

VII

TEUCHTERSHARDS

The gale which I had feared was going to blow did not materialise, but a drizzling soaking mist wafted down the sound and the cloud was so low that nothing of interest could be seen. In spite of this I spent most of the voyage on deck, hanging disconsolately over the rail or pacing up and down in what little walking space was available; for I could not bear the steamer's cramped and stuffy public rooms, still crowded at this season with holidaymakers and rendered insupportable by children running constantly here and there. It was early afternoon when we reached the island; the mist had lifted by this time and the clouds were beginning to scatter and break up. I discovered on enquiry that Teuchtershards was only four or five miles distant, and as my luggage was not heavy I decided to walk.

About two miles up the coast road I came to a lodge where a fairly wide dirt track headed across the moor by the side of a burn in the direction of the hills. There was no immediate sign of life at the lodge so I did not bother to stop and announce myself there; my bag was proving more of a nuisance than I had bargained for and I was anxious to reach the house as soon as possible. After a mile or two the road entered some woods, and in due course rhododendron bushes indicated that Teuchtershards was at hand. I was already very tired when at last I came upon it quite unexpectedly, sprawled beyond a broad lawn, with the hills, cleft by the burn which swept round the mansion to the left, rising steeply just behind. The house seemed built to give the impression that history and tradition had left their rich marks upon its walls, but I judged that it dated only from the middle or end of the last century. It was basically a three-storey building, its construction complicated however by a number of wings and turrets haphazardly thrown up at various times above and beyond the main fabric. As I trudged up the gravel path which bisected the lawn and led up to the main entrance, I had the sensation that many appraising eyes were scrutinising me from the long rows of windows, and I lowered my own eyes defensively, conscious of the loud scrunching of my feet which violated the silence.

My first ring at the bell produced no response, so I tried again; I was beginning to feel uneasy when at length a jolly, bustling old woman appeared and apologised for the delay. I explained who I was and she told me that she was Nanny, and that I was to come away in.

'You'll be seeing the factor nae doot,' she said, 'he's got all your instructions. But I'll make you feel at hame'. Her reference to the factor seemed to me to be accompanied by a kind of sniff of disapproval; but before I had time to ask her any questions she took my bag and disappeared at a spanking pace, clippety-clopping with tiny but thunderous steps across the polished wooden floor. I was left alone in a dim, galleried hall, silent as the grave and enlivened at various points by stags' heads and family portraits, which in the half-light it was not always easy to distinguish from one another. Opposite the front door was an impressive fireplace, and above it an immense oil-painting depicting the Gadarene swine tumbling over the cliff: those at the rear charging forward, their eyes rolling in madness, others near the edge of the precipice snorting in terror as they sighted the void and exerted themselves in vain efforts to pull up in time, while the unfortunate leaders plunged head over heels in droves, trotters flaying the air and curly tails thrashing in porcine confusion. Perhaps it represented the predicted destiny of the family Sykes-Buffington.

I suppose I sat staring at the epic painting in a kind of fascinated dwalm for about twenty minutes, too exhausted to move, as I awaited further developments. Eventually the factor appeared from the opposite direction from that in which Nanny had departed. He was a sallow, unsmiling fellow of about forty, a Lowlander and city-bred by the look and sound of him. He seemed to be on his dignity; probably my presence at Teuchtershards was an unmitigated nuisance to him. He explained to me in precise and formal terms that Viscount Gadarene had had to make an unforeseen trip to London, and would not be returning until the eve of the shooting-party in four days' time; his Lordship's apologies were conveyed to me, and I was invited to dine with him and Lady Gadarene on the evening of his arrival, by which time my work should be completed. Meanwhile I was to proceed with the valuation of the library; all my needs would be attended to, and it was hoped that I would ask for anything I wanted and feel thoroughly at home.

It has to be said that the factor's attitude to me did little to promote this final desideratum, for he made it clear that he was devoting time to my comfort and entertainment only because he had been instructed to do so. His first duty was to show me over the house, and he performed it with an air of weariness kept in check by a scrupulous sense of duty. He was a pompous man, but seemed to suffer from an inferiority complex, and I had the impression that he was adopting a special way of talking which he thought proper to employ when addressing an intellectual. Why he should have thought of me as an intellectual God only knows, but that was my impression. When he wanted to make a definitive statement he would sometimes behave as though he were delivering a speech, making use of carefully chosen, clearly enunciated and somewhat recondite phraseology, and puffing himself up as he spoke. He always referred to people as persons and to cars as vehicles, and spoke not of houses being sold but of properties changing hands; and if he wanted to convey the idea 'We expect to get more than £100 for these books', he would say, 'It is anticipated that these items will realise a sum in excess of One Hundred Pounds.' All this excess verbiage did little to recommend him to me.

The tour of Teuchtershards took a long time. Only a small proportion of the rooms were ever actually lived in, the rest of the vast rambling property being maintained as a kind of museum to house the art treasures collected by various Gadarenes over several generations. Many of these were without question very impressive, but they had been jumbled and crowded together without thought or taste; the innumerable rooms seemed quite uncared for, dust was everywhere, and the predominance of dark-coloured velvet in the draperies and furniture coverings contributed to a dingy, down-at-heels atmosphere accentuated by the failing light, and oddly at variance with the quality of the paintings, antiques and ornaments which abounded in every apartment. The factor, apparently, had no criteria of judgment at his disposal to indicate the worth of these but to ascribe to each of them a monetary value; the bombardment of figures to which I was subjected soon overwhelmed me, and I quickly ran out of phrases and epithets adequate to convey an appropriate degree of appreciation, and had to resort to little grunts of enthusiastic delight. These failed to impress the factor, who became more openly resentful as the tour progressed, and was obviously looking for an opportunity to put me down. He eventually got it. We came to a room which was almost completely occupied by the most enormous table I have ever seen, and this table was covered from end to end with correspondence. It seemed that Viscount Gadarene never threw a letter away, but simply allowed his mail to accumulate, quite neatly but endlessly and without any apparent principle of order, upon this table. While the factor was rambling on about the portraits on the wall I allowed my eyes to flit idly over some of these letters. The factor, suddenly aware of what I was up to, broke off in the middle of his monologue to inform me icily that he had been brought up in the belief that it was bad form to read other persons' letters.

'Were you?' I replied briskly. 'I'm glad to hear it.'

No, that is not true. That is what I ought to have said, but in fact I was too taken aback to summon the necessary presence of mind. In reality I blushed for shame and stammered out some excuse about wanting to see whether the crest on the notepaper was the same as the one on the books, which wouldn't have taken in a percipient child of two, far less a factor who could talk to intellectuals. It was an unqualified victory for the factor, and one from which I did not recover that day. A great weariness came over me soon after that, all the strain of my two days' travelling and two sleepless nights overwhelmed me, and I begged humbly and meekly to be shown to my bedroom.

This proved to be in a wing of the building which was obviously only one rung above the servants' quarters, but it served me well enough. I took a hot bath and shortly afterwards Nanny brought me in an excellent meal on a tray. I took to Nanny at once, and unlike the factor she seemed to take to me also; during the days which followed she was to become quite a friend of mine. She was a busy, chattering little thing, rosy and wrinkled, never quiet and never still. She was not an islander but hailed from Nethy Bridge; she was nearly seventy and had been in service with the family for over fifty years, first as nanny to the Viscount and then to his children, and now as resident factotum here at Teuchtershards. Nanny's presence made me feel safe and secure in this odd and alien environment into which I had entered like a thief in the night. She and the factor, indeed, could not have affected my mind with more contrasting impressions.

After my meal I lay down on my bed to think. Whether or not as a result of exhaustion, my mind was in a state of turmoil and conflict. The news that Lord Gadarene was not to return until almost the time that I was due to depart was very disturbing to me, not least because I was aware that the information had immediately affected me with a profound sense of relief. I feared the erosion of my resolution. Walking around the gloomy house with the factor, it is true, I had experienced briefly a surge of confidence in my powers; with the opportunity to perfect my plans at my leisure undisturbed by the pressure of my victim's presence about me, I envisaged myself acting swiftly and decisively at the fateful moment. But later as I sat and chatted pleasantly with Nanny beside the fire, my mission had suddenly seemed ridiculous and unreal: the image of myself as a cold, single-minded and implacable man of action threatened to thaw out and disintegrate in the warmth. These fluctuations of my mood were generating an incipient panic. My very self-respect had become identified with a faith in my ability to carry through what I had resolved.

As I lay with my hands clasped behind my head, turning these matters over in my mind, I began to be aware of orchestral music playing somewhere in the distance. I strained my ears, and recognised the first movement of Mozart's 'Jupiter' Symphony. With delight I heard the little theme which had captivated me in my childhood so many years before, and to which I owed all my early devotion to music and my abortive dreams of a musical career. An impulse drove me out into the corridor, so that I could hear it more clearly and perhaps trace the source of the music. I was soon quite baffled. Following the sound, I wandered up and down the dimly-lit passages, peering into shadowy chambers and cocking my ear at the foot of eerie staircases; the music would advance and recede as I travelled, but never could I reach it; I would think again and again that I had found the right direction, only to hear the notes fading unexpectedly and to set off on a fresh trail. It was a ghostly and disorientating pursuit, and I began to fear that I would lose myself hopelessly in the strange building; I made my way uncertainly back to my bedroom and there listened puzzled but enraptured as the last notes of the symphony died away. A tremendous relaxation overtook me. I went straight to my bed, fell asleep at once and slept like a log; and though the wrinkle-nosed laundryman invaded my dreams once more, I awoke refreshed and vigorous in the brisk September morning.

I started my work in the library immediately after breakfast that day, and was soon deeply immersed in my task. Though not a very large library it was full of valuable and interesting material, and what had originally been nothing but an excuse to get myself to Teuchtershards gradually became an absorbing preoccupation. Situated on the middle floor of the house to the rear, and commanding a view of the steep heathery hillside with the burn tumbling down through a little wooded glen, the fine old room was a pleasant place to work; it was constructed on two levels, the gallery having an impressive balustrade of carved wood with representations of mythical and emblematic beasts projecting at regular intervals. I remained all morning hard at work, and at various intervals I again heard music, but with no further enlightenment as to its source. Assuming that it was emanating from a single point, it seemed very odd that it should be audible in such widely separated parts of the house; and at times it appeared to me that the strains must be coming from outside. When Nanny brought my lunch into me at noon I asked her who it was in Teuchtershards who had such excellent taste in classical music. She chuckled away to herself, shaking her head.

'Away wi' ye, laddie, there's nae music here! Wha wad play it, dae ye think? There's naebody here but you an' me an' the factor, an' *he's* no musical! It's just pleasant dreams ye've been having!'

She chuckled away quietly for a while, but it struck me that in spite of her protestations my question had not come at all as a surprise to Nanny. I decided to pursue the subject no further with her; instead, the weather being fresh and autumnal, I set off in an attempt to track down the mystery out of doors, for the music was in the air once more, familiar but now eluding the grasp of my memory. Outside the sounds seemed fainter than in the house, but oddly enough they now came with a stronger sense of direction, and I took a track leading over the shoulder of the hill to the south-west, at first a rough path but soon no more than a sheep-track. Once over the rise I looked down on a deep inlet of the sea, with broken cliffs rising from a beach of sand and rock. The path wound down tortuously by way of a cleft to a spur of rock projecting into the sea; beyond it on my left hand the cliffs swept back in a semi-circle, deeply penetrated by a succession of caves, and enclosing a sandy beach approachable only by the route I had taken.

I wandered onto this beach, finding myself surrounded by the strangest forms of natural architecture. Everywhere the rock was eroded into odd twisted shapes suggestive of animate figures, and in the middle of the beach was raised a triumphal arch of three enormous pillars. The elusive music, while it still persisted, was no longer separable from the surging roar of the sea, and seemed less a human music than an expression or emanation of the pervasive atmosphere of this place to which it had drawn me. The character of this atmosphere might be described as a vigilant, intelligent calm; analogous to that sense of simplicity lying at the heart of complexity, into which we can sometimes be granted an insight in drink. The tide was far out; I strayed about, staring up at the pillars and peering into the gloom of the caves, not thinking of anything but lost in an almost substanceless musing, unaware that time was passing. It was only when a chilly breeze got up and stirred me out of my dwalm that I realised that I should long ago have been back at work in the library.

I was still anxious to arrive at some rational explanation of the puzzling music, and when the following afternoon as I was coming in from my walk I caught sight of the factor approaching from the direction of the stables, I hailed him, in spite of his obvious reluctance to be distracted from whatever business he was occupied with, and broached the matter with him. I had not expected friendliness but neither was I prepared for the response that was forthcoming. A contortion of fury disfigured his features and for a moment I thought he was going to hit me; controlling this impulse with obvious reluctance, he answered me in tones of withering contempt.

'It does not form part of my remit,' he said precisely, 'to furnish an explanation for every hallucination experienced by persons temporarily in the employ of this estate. To play nursemaid is not one of the facets of my appointment. An approach to Nanny would have greater pertinence in this context.'

Having delivered himself of this accomplished salvo he turned on his heel and stamped off in the direction from which he had come. I retired greatly troubled, indeed shaking in a fine tremor in all my limbs; for in the instant before he succeeded in mastering his explosion of temper his expression had reflected unmistakably the malignant, implacable stare of the wrinkle-nosed laundryman. That night, when I suffered my now habitually recurring nightmare, the laundryman was entirely confounded in my consciousness with the malevolent factor, rather than with Mr. Raith as hitherto. I did not escape from him at the chimney-stack, moreover, but engaged with him in a bitter grapple, he encircling my chest with his arms in a vicelike grip which threatened to force all the air from my lungs forever. I awoke in a terrible paralysis, unable to stir a limb or make the slightest sound; and then, with a noise of rushing water in my ears, began to descend again into what I knew would be a sleep of death if I did not succeed in rousing myself in time. At the final moment I was released with a violent snap, and lay with my heart thundering from terror and exhaustion, as though my struggle had been with flesh and blood rather than with the fleeting phantoms of my own mind.

The following day however I made a discovery which fascinated me and lightened my mood. In a corner of the library at the near end of the gallery, just to the left of the little iron staircase which led up there, I found an illustrated edition of *The Ancient Mariner*, dating from 1848. The illustrations had been taken from woodcuts, and were executed with masterly draughtsmanship and exquisite sensitivity of taste. I had seen many attempts before to give pictorial form to the evocative and powerful images of the poem, but none seemed to me to have captured the projections of the poet's inner eye so well as these. Especially illuminating was the interpretation of the Mariner's blessing of the water snakes, when the foul and slimy monsters of the deep are revealed to his renewed eyes as beauteous expressions of life. I would stand gazing spellbound at this picture for half an hour at a stretch, unconscious of the passage of time and forgetful of the job on which I was supposed to be engaged. It was fortunate that the bulk of my work was done before I came upon this book, for otherwise the valuation of Lord Gadarene's library would probably have remained incomplete to this day.

Three days passed almost without my being aware of their passage. I was not unconscious of the fact that my absorption in my official work was a device by means of which I was shutting out the conflict raging within me over my true purpose for being at Teuchtershards. Every time I saw the odious factor I had the quite irrational impression that the hostile looks which he was always bending upon me were intended as a reproach for my procrastination; while my every conversation with my good angel Nanny seemed to remove me further from a state of mind in which I could bend my will to my duty. Daily I resolved to settle down to serious preparation when I was alone in my room in the evening; but always the ubiquitous and untraceable music would descend upon my ears, soothing my consciousness and lowering my senses into an enclosing soporific warmth. Before I was aware of what was happening I would be so irresistibly and yet pleasantly overcome by drowsiness that mind would drift away into nebulous and whimsical fancies, and I would have no alternative but to roll into bed, where I invariably sank at once into the deepest sleep. Only my hideous dream, recurring night after night with relentless insistence, kept recalling my fickle conscience to the reason for my presence at Teuchtershards.

On the afternoon of the day before Viscount Gadarene was due to return, I admitted to myself that all hopes of perfecting in advance a detailed plan for the assassination would have to be abandoned. I would be obliged instead to rely entirely on my nerve and resourcefulness, to be ever on the alert for my opportunity, and to recognise it and grasp it fearlessly when it came. There might indeed be advantages to be gained from such a necessity. Plans could go wrong in quite unexpected ways and leave the most thorough tactician floundering without resource; but the authority to seize the moment, the lightning reflex, the swift, unhesitating and unwavering confrontation with destiny, the sudden and decisive movement of the individual will as it lays its hold upon history—none of these things could in anyway be resisted.

In spite of all that I had learned of him from wee Tam I had been quite unable to form any consistent mental picture of my intended victim. This troubled me; when you are going to kill someone it is natural enough to want to know *who* it is that you will be dispatching from this life, and the teaching of E.V. Messer insisted that it was individuals who were to be executed for their misdeeds, not mere embodied ideals whose elimination would be solely a function of their assassins' egotism. I made up my mind therefore to learn what I could from Nanny about her employer's character and attributes, and when she came to remove my supper tray that evening I invited her to sit down and have a little chat.

I have to admit that what I heard from that excellent old person shook my preconceptions about the disposition of our decadent aristocrat not a little, though not entirely my resolve to wipe him from the face of the earth. At first Nanny would not be drawn on the subject: from my line of tentative questioning she must have inferred a degree of antagonism towards one whom she had after all raised from the cradle, and her sense of loyalty made her so wary that none of the meagre information she provided gave me any immediate impression of the man whom tomorrow I would be obliged to slay. I realised that the only way of getting some spontaneous expression of her feelings about him was by provoking her; so instead of moderating my approach I cunningly induced an explosive reaction from her by making my references to Lord Gadarene ever more ill-disposed, flagrantly insinuating and at the last grossly insulting. At length Nanny could take no more and burst into tears of aggrieved affection, and a passionate defence of her employer. I will not describe that scene, for to tell the truth I am heartily ashamed of it. It was a wicked and inexcusable thing that I had done, even though it had just the effect that I had intended. I managed at length to pacify and console Nanny by telling her that I had a genuine and honourable reason for testing her loyalty, but one which in the interests of her master I could not at that time disclose; I unreservedly praised her demonstration of her faithfulness, saying that her feelings did her the utmost credit and that the Viscount could feel proud to have been raised by such a nanny. She came around quite readily after that, with a show of reluctance it is true, but one which was soon submerged in gratitude and relief; and she told me a tale which disclosed the basis of her devotion to my victim-to-be.

Nanny, it seems, had a past. When she had first gone into service with the Sykes-Buffingtons as an under-nanny, before the First World War, she had been only fifteen, and the eldest son of the family, Hugh—'Big Shuie, we cried him'—at thirteen a mere two years her junior; Anthony Augustus, the present Viscount, being two or three years younger again. A bond of affection grew up between Hugh and Nanny, which in the course of a number of years blossomed into a fully developed, though naturally well concealed, romance. The time came when the heir to the title left Teuchtershards for the trenches, but not without having impregnated Nanny a short time before his departure; he was killed in action, in rather heroic circumstances, within a month, still unaware of the condition of the girl he had left behind him. Nanny's secret was eventually discovered, as such secrets generally are, and inevitably the Gadarenes were all for putting her on the first boat for the mainland so that she might have her child as far away from Teuchtershards as possible and trouble them no further. But she had one friend at court: Anthony Augustus, a lad of seventeen and now of course the future Lord Gadarene. To Nanny's surprise—for they had not previously hit it off very well together—he had pleaded passionately with his father that she should be allowed to remain in the household, and even to bring up her child as one of the family. The old Viscount, still grieving for his firstborn, was in a frame of mind to be indulgent towards his remaining son, and to such effect did the latter put his case that he prevailed upon his parents to allow Nanny to remain, although she was not permitted to keep her child, which was put out to adoption.

To the present Lord Gadarene, then, Nanny felt that she owed almost her very existence; for life outside Teuchtershards she was now scarcely able to conceive of as life in any real sense at all. Hence her touching and unshakeably loyal gratitude, which she would clearly maintain in the face of whatever criticisms of her benefactor could possibly be raised. Faults she was quite prepared to admit he had (though what these might be she resolutely refused to say); but for her none of them were of any significance beside what she owed to his intervention in the great crisis of her life.

When she finally hurried away with my tray after more than an hour's talk, Nanny left me in a most thoughtful and rather disturbed frame of mind. To learn, on the very eve of an assassination attempt, that one's intended victim has, even if a long time in the past, exhibited any redeeming or sympathetic human qualities, is far from encouraging, as may well be imagined. I had naturally hoped that she would condemn his Lordship as a monster of crass and insentient egotism, an unqualified moral barbarian. That would have made my task less exacting. However, I realised well enough that in a calling such as the one I had chosen there was no room for sentiment; so I hardened my heart and did my best to expunge from my mind the feelings stirred in my by Nanny's tale.

VIII

THE CRISIS

The following evening at about seven o'clock I presented myself, handsomely fitted out in my archaic dinner jacket but trembling with apprehension beneath it, in the spacious parlour where the factor, with a surly air and probably greatly to his distaste, introduced me to Lord Gadarene. The factor was apparently going to dine with us, to my acute discomfort, of his silent, exacting presence and of his stealthy and insinuating gaze.

The Viscount approached me smiling broadly, his hand outstretched in welcome. He was a tall and upright figure of about sixty-five, with silvery grey hair and the commanding features and distinguished bearing once obligatory in male members of his social class. He introduced me in turn to his wife, the frail but talkative little Lady Penelope, and a long-haired sullen youth who proved to be Hector, his younger son, a student at St. Andrews University. Hector skulked in the background and mumbled his greetings in a gauche, off-hand sort of way. The factor meanwhile was hanging around on the fringes of the party, no doubt anxious to keep his malicious eye on me unobserved, and hopeful of seeing me shown up in a bad light in front of the Gadarenes. The Viscount and his lady paid him very little attention, Lord Gadarene merely indicating with a 'Thank you, Sellar' when he wanted the glasses refilled, as if the fellow had been not a factor but a butler.

As sherry was drunk I began, in an attempt to overcome my anxiety, to tell Lord Gadarene about my work on the library; but he raised his hand to stop me, saying that tomorrow morning would be quite time enough to talk business and that tonight I was to relax and enjoy myself after my labours.

'Tell me, though, Mr. Pagan,' he continued pleasantly, 'the shop which your firm now occupies—did it not at one time house the premises of old Murray, the locksmith. I dare say that would be long before your day, though,' he rambled on as I made no sign of recognition, 'I'm talking about when I lived in Edinburgh as a young man, forty years ago or more. But that's the shop that old man Murray had, I'm certain. A nice old man he was too. You must remember him, Penelope?' he added, turning to his wife for corroboration.

'Indeed I do, a jolly plump smiling little man. I remember him very well.'

'Plump and smiling? Murray?' The Viscount exuded astonishment. 'That's the first I've heard of it. I would have described him as tall, dignified and thin as a rake. You're thinking of Paterson the painter, further down the street.'

'No, no, Tony, I'm not thinking of Paterson. I know Paterson perfectly well, I knew him throughout my girlhood, and Murray too—they were both small and plump but Murray was plumper than Paterson.'

'Murray plumper than Paterson! The thing's fantastic!' cried Lord Gadarene. 'Heavens above, woman, Paterson was so fat he could scarcely bend to tie his bootlaces! In fact I *remember* stopping to tie his laces up for him one day in Pitt Street when they came undone and he couldn't do them up again!'

'I recall your telling me *that* all right,' riposted Lady Penelope triumphantly, 'but that wasn't Paterson, that was Bennett the butcher.'

The Viscount shook his head sadly, with mock resignation. 'Bennett the butcher, my dear girl, was dead before you were born. And as for Murray the locksmith, he was so thin you could almost see through him.'

'Then we are obviously not talking about the same Murray,' retorted his lady sturdily. 'The Murray I knew was plump and jovial.'

'It *is* the same Murray,' insisted Lord Gadarene with a terrible smile, fury struggling with manners for the mastery of his features, 'and he may have been plump and jovial when you knew him, but when *I* knew him he was tall and gaunt.'

Fortunately at this point Nanny entered to announce that dinner was served. I was very glad to see her. The Viscount made a great deal of show of shaking his head knowingly to himself as he ushered me through to the vast, gloomy and overfurnished dining-room, all of its pieces groaning beneath the weight of the valuable silver with which they were laden.

'And are you married, Mr. Pagan?' asked Lady Penelope charmingly when we were seated and digging into our avocado pears.

'No, Lady Gadarene, I'm afraid not,' said I.

'Oh, do call me Lady Penelope,' she pleaded.

'Feel free to call me Horatio,' I mumbled in return. She raised her hands in delight.

'Horatio! Isn't that nice. How seldom we hear such grand old names these days. I take it you were named for our dear Lord Nelson?'

'Scarcely, Lady Penelope,' I explained, permitting myself just the suggestion of a satiric intonation. 'This is how it came about. It happened that when my father saw me for the first time, mewling and puking in my mother's arms, for some reason he fainted on the spot. When he had been revived my mother exclaimed to him, with teasing affection, "There are more things in heaven and earth, Horatio, than are dreamt of in your philosophy." She had once played Ophelia in an amateur production, you see, and she knew her *Hamlet*. My parents started jocularly referring to me as Horatio after that, and the name stuck. It has proved the bane of my life.'

'Well I dare say it has been a nuisance to you, but what a sweet story! And do you intend to marry, Horatio?' she pursued, harping back irritatingly to her original question. But the Viscount cut in with authoritative rudeness before I had a chance to reply.

'I'll give you one piece of advice, Horatio,' he said. 'If and when you *do* decide to get married, don't marry outside your own class. It never works out. I'll tell you a true story. I had an uncle, a younger brother of my mother's, who married out of his class. He was a brash young student at Oxford at the time, went on a weekend's outing to Brighton, met a barmaid there, fell head over heels in love with her, married within a month, all that sort of stuff. Well, she led him a hell of a life. He would never admit it you see, because the family had of course utterly opposed the match and his pride wouldn't let him admit that it hadn't worked out. She led him a hell of a life, just wore him out eventually—killed him, not to put too fine a point on it. She simply drove him to his grave. Always nagging at him, rowing, throwing things at him and so on, she even used to break records over his head. But he wouldn't leave her because of their daughter—he was very, very fond of his little daughter, completely and utterly devoted to her in fact.' He shook his head in sorrowful remembrance. 'In the end he died a very tragic death, his heart simply gave out one afternoon after a children's party. They found him sitting dead in the nursery, with a balloon tied to his chair and a broken doll at his feet.' He shook his head again, contemplatively. 'So there's a lesson to be learned from that story. Never marry out of your class. Isn't that right, Nanny?' he flashed suddenly at the old woman, who was hovering in the background, helping with the serving of the meal.

'Oh ay, sir, you're right enough there,' said Nanny obligingly, though in some confusion at these tactless words. The factor sniggered audibly.

'It's advisable not to bed down out of your class, too, wouldn't you say, Nanny?' he asked coolly.

It was the first time he had spoken during the meal, and for an instant there was an utterly concussed silence. The temerity, malice and vulgarity of those words were alike so remarkable that the mind revolted against the evidence of the ears. It was in fact an appalling blunder on the factor's part, and must have arisen from the unbearably protracted suppression of some murderous resentment, suddenly incapable any longer of containing itself. In fact, the frustrated venom could just be detected in a slight wobble of the furiously controlled voice. Lord Gadarene ceased eating but did not withdraw his eyes from his plate.

'Get out, Sellar,' he said without expression.

For an instant the factor remained seated, then white as a spectre he rose and left the room without a word. As he went out of the door he cast back over his shoulder one tortured, indescribably bitter look which took in the whole table but seemed peculiarly intended for Nanny and myself. I glanced over to where that old lady stood, and saw almost with joy her dignified, unbowed but unexulting little person, her face slightly flushed at the cheekbones but otherwise unmarked by what had passed. It was almost as if she personally had defeated the factor without lifting a hand or speaking a syllable, by sheer force of right. With his departure an intolerable weight was at once lifted from my shoulders. Everything seemed more human at that table thereafter.

'There, you see, Nanny agrees with me; *he* won't agree, though,' said his Lordship, continuing as if the interruption had never occurred and indicating Hector, who was attacking a roll with mute savagery.

'He agrees with very little of what his old father has to say at present, since they have been filling his head full of odd ideas at that university. He is very much to the left these days, I believe.'

'And you are very much to the right these days,' replied Hector crassly, spoiling for a fight. His father did not deign to reply, so he was obliged to say something else. 'My ideas are my own, anyway,' he snapped. 'No one filled my head with them except myself.'

'Whosoever they are, they're pretty funny ideas,' said his father sagely, 'but I have no doubt that time will take care of them as it always does.'

'Time? What has time got to do with it?' asked Hector without looking up from his food.

'Time and change happeneth to them all,' quoted the Viscount pompously, as if in answer to the question.

'You'll have to enlighten me further. I may be stupid,' replied the son. 'It's "time and chance" anyway,' he added smugly.

This conversation was just the sort of thing which I had earlier been hoping to hear, confirming as it did the preconceptions I had formed about the Viscount, which needed to be confirmed if the planned assassination was to be justified. Earlier in the meal, with the eye of the factor ever upon me, I had been conscientiously screwing my courage to the sticking-point; but his departure had relieved me so much that I was now in a light-hearted, almost giddy frame of mind utterly unconducive to political concerns. The good bottle of red wine which accompanied the main course was also not without its effect on me, so that my mission was once again thrust from the forefront of my mind, and the meal proceeded pleasantly enough amid vacuous small talk.

'Have you seen my new lawnmower?' Lord Gadarene asked me as the duck was taken away. 'The gardener had it out on the front lawn this morning.'

'I have,' I replied with as much enthusiasm as I could muster. 'It seems a very handsome machine.'

'It's a magnificent machine,' said the Viscount, swelling with pride and gratification. 'I've never known one that made such a fine job of the lawn. I can recommend it most strongly—and it wasn't dear.'

'It's leaking petrol just now, though,' put in Hector with some malice. 'I've discovered the cause of it but it'll have to be fixed professionally.'

'Have you been fiddling about with that mower?' his father shot at him, turning the colour of a turkey-cock.

'No,' said Hector absolutely tonelessly and without emphasis. He was not going to give his father the satisfaction of any reassuring protestations of innocence.

Lord Gadarene began to eat his pudding, obviously far from contented. But suddenly his colour rose again, he clattered his spoon down on the plate, and with his mouth still full, muttering an incoherent excuse, he got up and almost ran out of the room. A few seconds later we could hear his feet scrunching in haste across the gravel outside. Lady Penelope raised her eyebrows and directed a quizzical look at her son, but he was concentrating furiously on his pudding, so she redirected it as myself, and I returned it with a shrug and an embarrassed smile.

'He's gone raving mad!' Hector exploded. 'He's been going slowly off his head for years, and now at last he's emerged as a fully-fledged raving lunatic!'

'Now, now, calm down,' said his mother mildly.

'What did he think he'd be able to see in this light anyway, the idiot?' shouted Hector as we heard the crunch of the peer's returning footsteps. The old gentleman appeared somewhat mollified by his excursion, nevertheless.

'You just be careful of that machine, it's worth a great deal of money,' he said to his son almost confidingly, and with a hint of good humour, as he resumed his seat.

It was at this point that an extraordinary and quite unexpected thing happened. Quite without my own volition a huge and uncontrollable surge of sympathy for the old Viscount swept through my veins. There was something so touchingly and pathetically human about the whole scene: his ridiculous and exaggerated concern for his machine, his mounting anxiety, the callous and unfeeling behaviour of the son of whom in spite of everything he was obviously proud and fond; his almost absurd return, with his damaged confidence restored, and his rather sheepish attempt to justify his undignified dash out of the room: all of this struck home to me instantly in the sharpest way and my heart went out to him with an unbidden movement of something approaching love. That this should happen was quite unaccountable to me; I suppose that those with religious inclinations might term it grace. In that moment, too, I understood with immediate and absolute finality that I could never carry out the deed to which I was supposed to be committed. It was simply not in me: I was not Raskolnikov. The heroic qualities of mind and spirit which I believed to be necessary for such a calling, and which I had successfully persuaded myself that I possessed, maintaining the conviction with all the certainty and assurance normally granted only to religious fanatics concerning their own salvation, were not in me either. I would never be a Brutus or a Charlotte Corday or even a Lee Harvey Oswald. It had all been in the mind. I could no more carry out an assassination that I could ever write a great symphony.

My first reaction to this discovery was an overpowering desire to laugh. I did not laugh aloud, but I chuckled away inordinately deep down inside myself. A tremendous relaxation loosened all my limbs, and the wine I had drunk went instantaneously to my head. I wanted to embrace those ridiculous people and tell them that I loved them. Fortunately I managed to restrain this impulse, for otherwise I would probably have been thrown out of the house at once as a madman. I next realised that from this point in my life onwards I could begin to enjoy myself. A huge weight of responsibility was lifted from my shoulders. I wanted to begin enjoying myself at once, and I was even prepared to start doing it there and then at dinner with the Sykes-Buffingtons—it had come to that.

I was aware though, somewhere in the recesses of my mind, that this happy reaction took its character partly at least from the quantity of wine I had consumed. It was underlaid by the cold, still certainty that I had at last pulled down the pillars of my arrogance, perhaps of my self-belief; but I did not yet know whether their collapse might bring down upon my head the entire shaky edifice of my life. As this consciousness took root within me I involuntarily began to sober up; and when dinner was over I excused myself as soon as I decently could, explaining that I was very tired and anxious to get to bed.

I did not go there however, for I needed to think, and only when I am walking can I think clearly. Instead I left the house and took the path over the shoulder of the hill, drawn to that suggestive, almost animate stretch of coast whither I had pursued the mysterious music. The night was cool and by no means very dark, and a three-quarter moon hung before me over the hill. As I approached a stile in a dyke I was unexpectedly pulled up short. A figure rose up from behind the wall, barring my way. My heart lunged in my chest—it was the wrinkle-nosed laundryman, or the malevolent factor, or the enigmatic Mr. Raith, or all or none of them. God only knows. After the initial shock was past I felt no fear.

'Spineless cur!' the phantom hissed. 'Are you forgetful already of your sacred undertaking?'

'Let me pass, sir,' I replied with superb confidence, 'for you're a bad man entirely.'

I stood my ground with fearless insolence, and after a few moments' confrontation the wretched creature fell back cringing and snarling, visibly shrunken and reduced in stature and quite unable to withstand the power of my will. I negotiated the stile without let or hindrance and passed on without looking back. Soon I had descended the precipitous route to the shore and crossed the spur of broken rocks which enclosed the beach.

The animation of the place, though very strong, seemed less friendly than in the light of noonday. The cliffs towered black above me, the dark recesses of the caves might have harboured monsters, the pillars of the triple arch seemed silent, watchful giants casting upon me a searching but unfathomable gaze. No music sounded now but the monotonous music of the sea, upon which the sailing moon cast a cold, eerie effulgence. A terrible gloom descended upon me: never had I felt so utterly alone. At that moment I would almost have welcomed the company of the persecuting spirit whom I had but now banished from my sight. I was alone now with my self, naked and unprotected, for the first time in my life. An awful dead blankness infested my mind, obliterating thought as a pillow might smother away the life of a sleeping victim of murder by night. I was groping in the blind darkness for the new life which would not be revealed, and by no means could I conjure it into a vital form.

F

I wandered up and down upon that beach for I do not know how long, my head sunk upon my chest, heedless of where I was, a lost and homeless soul.

When I again became aware of my surroundings I found myself a prisoner. The rising tide, to which I had given no thought, had entirely covered the spur of rock and cut off all retreat from the isolated beach. Even as I had paced the beach I had been unconsciously giving way before the advancing waters, and now I stood at the very base of the cliff, in front of the mouths of the caves. It was dark and cold and the moon, which I could not see from where I was, must have disappeared behind the crest of the hill, for its light vanished swiftly from the face of the sea, though the stars still shone coldly in the firmament. I felt no fear, no emotion of any kind, nothing at all did I feel except exhaustion. I crept into the deepest cave on my hands and knees until I came to a place where the sand was dry in the inmost cranny, and there I lay down, huddling myself up as best I could against the cold, my back to the dank wall. I hoped indeed that the tide never entirely filled this cave, but in truth I cared little; and almost at once, resigning myself to passivity, I fell into an unstirring sleep.

Sometime during that night I began to dream once more the nightmare which had tormented me without respite since the night in the hostel in Glasgow. Again I was standing on the sinister pathway, conscious of a foul enveloping horror moving from all sides to entrap me; and again against my will I was compelled, slowly but inevitably, to turn my head to the right. There as ever was my spine-chilling adversary, poised to launch himself with murderous fingers at my throat. I turned and fled, and on the pursuit went as it always did, up on the rooftops and on to that fatal chinmey-stack. In despair I turned and braced myself to face death. My enemy was before me; and for all the loathesome wrinkle-nosed mask that he wore I knew him beyond doubting to be myself. He drew the scouting-knife inconceivably slowly from within the folds of his black coat, and his cold mocking gaze was unbearably bent upon me. This was the point at which I normally threw myself off the roof: but now I stood stock still, waiting for my foul double to strike. He struck—and I caught his wrist as the knife quivered an inch from my heart. A tense, silent, appalling struggle followed, in such torturingly slow motion that it seemed that it might never cease. Slowly, slowly, intolerably slowly, I forced my enemy round until our positions were reversed, and I turned the knife back upon his heart, looking into his eyes all the time. I felt the point penetrate his black serge coat, then his jacket and shirt, I seemed to feel its first cold pricking against his white skin; I felt it penetrate skin and flesh and muscle, and work its way through the rib-cage towards the heart. But I knew that it had penetrated the source of his life only when I saw the demonic grin freeze by moments on his face, and his scornful eyes glaze gradually into sightlessness. Then he sank backwards, still infinitely slowly and without the ghost of a sound, off the knife; I felt it disengage from his flesh before he toppled past the corner of the chimney-stack and fell head over heels, slowly and gracefully yet, down the sloping roof and dropped off the edge. I leaned forward and saw him crumpled on the ground below, a shapeless inert mass that might have been nothing but a black serge coat. The dream dwindled imperceptibly into forgetfulness and I slept on.

When I awoke the sun was long risen and the day seemed joyful. I crawled stiffly from my resting-place, into which the sun had penetrated to within three feet of where I had lain; and as, standing upon the drying beach in a fresh breeze, I stretched my limbs and gazed westwards at the ebbing waves, a swift dart of joy entered my heart. The music was returned. Whether the source lay in the waves or in the heavens or in the echoing halls of my own mind, the tremendous opening notes of Beethoven's Fifth Symphony sounded out in that place. Up and down I strode with the great music moving in waves through my mind, and the most various emotions arose in my spirit as the huge rhythms beat in my ears and their resonance extended endlessly. The music spoke of bitter pain and endurance and of obscure and unsung wrongs, and beyond the fate of individuals it seemed to speak of the sad history of my unhappy nation, of deprivation and killing poverty and exile and the murderous toil which had been the lot of so many of its people for so long. But it spoke too of the misery of the spirit self-transcendent at the last, rising triumphantly above itself in affirmation. So I paced on unheedingly and the music continued to rise and swell in my mind until it embodied at last the sufferings of all the children of men and of all God's creatures. For a fleeting moment among those sounds I caught a glimpse of the unsurpassed vision of human love, transcending all odds and circumstances, all pain and loss, in a comprehensive embrace which would unite all the creatures of the earth; and in the contemplation of this desired end my pride fell for an instant away from me and I stood humble for the first time. An obscure and difficult path seemed to offer itself before me and a tired, tentative peace entered my heart.

It was in the morning of my departure. When I returned to Teuchtershards I bathed and packed my bag, then sought out Nanny for a farewell chat. I did not tell her of how I had spent the night, but I believe she understood something of what had taken place within me; and perhaps she had more to do with that than I will ever know. At the very least I came under the influence of her serene kindness, and that I am not likely ever to forget. Handel's *Water Music* wafted pleasantly up and down the corridors as I made my way downstairs, as if to wish me a safe and peaceful voyage that afternoon.

Lord Gadarene accompanied me a little way down the drive when I set of to walk to the steamer, I explained to him fully and clearly my conclusions of the subject of his library, and he expressed himself eminently satisfied with the work I had done. When I had thanked him for his hospitality, I remarked how extraordinary it was to recall that I had come to Teuchtershards with the firm intention of stabbing him in the back.

'Why, you cold-blooded young devil!' he exclaimed with a laugh. This was most unjust; I have a warm and passionate nature. But I don't think he really believed me anyway.

IX

REPENTANCE AND RETURN

It was a fine, clear day as the steamer sailed down the sound, with a breeze that was almost chill now that summer was giving way to autumn. I leaned abstractedly over the rail, watching the foam churning and subsiding and bubbling into slow dissolution in the wake of the boat. I was in a contemplative mood. I had lain down a heavy burden with the realisation that I had been mistaken about my destiny, but I understood that I had lost something too. Not that I had any real regrets; but I felt somehow bereaved, as if I had lost an old friend whose companionship had given form and substance to my life. It seemed a very long time since I had read the fateful work of E.V. Messer and had begun to conceive of myself as one of the exceptional spirits of whom he had written. To be without that inner support would take a little getting used to.

Yet already, when I thought about them, the events of the past months began to seem slightly unreal. This feeling was to gain ground in the days and weeks that followed, until in the end I began to wonder in a self-deprecating kind of way whether there might not be much in that sequence which I had only imagined. Had the enigmatic Mr. Raith really called at Bookless and Bone's that evening, and had a book called *Famous Assassins* appeared mysteriously on the shelves as if in answer to some inner summons? Had it really been that the wrinkle-nosed laundryman had haunted me in so many far-flung places? There was no doubt that I had been to Teuchtershards; but it sometimes appeared to me that I had simply been sent there on business by my Uncle Sean, rather than that I had gone on my own initiative in order to carry out a carefully-prepared scheme to assassinate its owner. But it was only with the passage of time that these doubts began to assert themselves, and I am inclined on the whole to attribute them to the not uncommon and perhaps quite forgivable defence mechanism by the aid of which human beings manage to adapt themselves to unwelcome realities. Because I had failed in my mission, and been obliged to admit that I was not constituted in the way that I had believed, there was a tendency for me to play down the whole business, think of it as a mere aberration, pretend that it had never really possessed the importance or even the authenticity which at the time had been unchallengeable. So at any rate it appears to me.

Such considerations were not in my mind that day on the steamer; a marked but not unpleasant weariness had come over me, which affected me with a desire not to think, to adopt from now on a passive and accepting attitude towards experience. I no longer wanted to exercise my wits in thinking abstractly about my own destiny or anyone else's; and words appeared to me as useless, contradictory and superficial. I was still under the influence of the unexplained music which had cushioned my senses during those days at Teuchtershards, and I surrendered myself again in my mind to its supportive power. In thus turning back to the old love of my childhood I was not unconscious of a form of regression; I gave myself up to the spirit of music as a tired child to sleep in its mother's arms: there was no exactment there. On turning my back on the universe of ideas I had a sense of giving up a struggle, of reverting to a simpler and more primitive form of spiritual being. For if music expressed all that was deepest in the life of man, if all that in daily life was subject to opacity and confusion found therein its clear and unequivocal expression, yet language was the tool and symbol of man's forward thrust: 'and now nothing will be restrained to them, which they have imagined to do.' To turn away from the world of language and ideas in favour of a retrenchment towards those underlying verities which only music could express was thus to sacrifice intellectual struggle and striving to the extreme longing for spiritual rest.

I spent that night in Brieston, at the same hotel where I had suffered so horrible a torment at the hands of the wrinkle-nosed laundryman, and it was amazing how altered for me was the aspect of the whole place. I still had a week of my holiday left; and so pleasant did I find the little town that I seriously considered remaining there for several days. What chiefly changed my mind was an unexpected and overpowering desire to see my father again and to be reconciled with him. This feeling came over me very suddenly, and at the same time it seemed unaccountable, but also irresistible. I decided therefore to take the rest of my holiday at home, and I caught a bus back to Edinburgh the following day.

It was as well that I did so. No sooner had I let myself into my flat on my return than there came a ring on the doorbell. It was my Uncle Sean, who had been waiting in the shop below in the slight hope that I might return that night after only a week away. My father was dying. In my obsession with my exalted plans I had forgotten about his illness almost as soon as my uncle had informed me of it, and indeed I had not given it another thought from that moment to this, my anxiety to see him being quite unconnected with any such thoughts. Having parted from the old man in anger nearly three years before, I had simply dismissed my progenitor from my life, and had callously thrown away without so much as a qualm the opportunity with which my uncle had presented me of making things right while I still could; and I had done so only to satisfy the pettiest kind of pride. Now, it might be too late.

For the first time in my life I felt utterly humbled as I stood there before my Uncle Sean, the memory of my arrogance on the occasion of our last meeting consuming me within. But he took no advantage whatsoever of my misery; no reference at all did he make to my refusal to visit my father before my departure, nor to my unfilial conduct during the past years. Instead, he was quietly helpful and sympathetic, and offered unostentatiously to drive me out to the manse straightaway. By no sign at all did he manifest even the slightest hint of smugness or satisfaction in relation to my obvious shame and discomfiture. Considering the way I had always treated him I think that this speaks for an element of something akin to nobility in my uncle's nature.

When we reached the manse, I was reunited with my mother, brother and sister; and again no words of reproach were passed, nor did any looks indicate that such words were being pointedly left unspoken. Even my brother Shugs, to whom I had always been particularly evilly disposed, welcomed me in the most open-hearted way; and again I was conscious of my extreme unworthiness. My father had cancer of the liver, which had advanced insidiously at first and for a long time had been left undiagnosed; then it had exploded catastrophically, and laid him low in the space of two or three weeks. His death was now near at hand. He had not been asking to see me, but I went up at once to his room.

There was no response to my knock on the door, so I entered with some apprehension and saw my father lying with his eyes closed and his arms stretched out on top of the bedclothes. He did not have the look of being asleep, but I knew that he was heavily sedated. He was terribly changed, though this came as no surprise to me. His large frame looked in a way larger because of the ghastly lack of flesh to cover it, and his skin was a sickening yellow; his pyjama sleeves had ridden up to reveal mottled patches on the pale arms. I noticed the thin, pinched look of his strong nose. When I spoke he opened his eyes and turned his head towards me, and appeared to recognise me; but he showed no sign of surprise, and I had no idea whether he any longer had any consciousness of the rift between us or of my long neglect. What sense of time and place he still retained I could not tell. I did not feel that there was any purpose in attempting now to heal that breach with words, or any possibility of it. I asked him how he was feeling, and he managed to say something in reply, but he had great difficulty in speaking. I went and sat in a chair by the window, and for a while tried to talk to him a little, about members of our family and about what I was doing with myself. He nodded from time to time and tried to smile, but I did not know how much he was taking in.

After some minutes I felt that it was time for me to go. I knew that it would be the last time that I would see him. I rose and stood by the bedside, and I felt that I wanted to make some final gesture. We did not go in much for physical expressions of affection in our family, and I do not think that I had touched my father, except to shake his hand, since I was a small child. Now I wanted to lay my hand for a moment on his arm, and as I made to do so he raised his hand from the bedclothes and gripped me below the elbow with as much strength as he had in him; I gripped his forearm in response. He was saying something which I could not make out, and I moved my ear closer to his mouth. 'A Roman handshake,' he said.

In the weeks that followed my father's death I thought much about those things in me which had made me wrong him, and not him alone but many of the people with whom I had had occasion to deal in my life. To say that I *thought* much is perhaps inaccurate, but I allowed a consciousness of these matters to be ever present in my mind, waking and sleeping, until I came to apprehend, obscurely and hesitantly enough at first, a little of their nature. I tried to be more understanding of my fellow-men. I had never really liked people very much, and had ever been quicker to see the bad in them than the good. Human beings had seemed to me in the main to be ugly, coarse and vulgar, and irredeemably banal if not corrupt. Perhaps they were, too; but I began to see at that time that things could be looked at from an alternative angle.

One day after a hard day at the bookshop I was relaxing in front of the fire with a can of beer, thinking about nothing in particular. I fell into a kind of doze, not true sleep but not full consciousness either. As I dozed it seemed to me that a procession was passing before my eyes, a parade of all the people who had played any part in my life, and of other anonymous faces too, in the midst of whom they moved; I, too, was there. Among them were many I had despised or wronged or held in low esteem, counting them as fit only to go on their bellies and eat the dust of the earth. Yet now my disgust was gone and I saw those people in a more generous light, as individual souls each striving in his or her own fashion towards a common goal, and there was a brightness on their features which belied the commonplaceness of their outward forms. Stripped now of their ignominy and ugliness—though the features were the same—their faces were alive with the ardent desires of their longing souls. The light on their faces was the effulgence which sprang from their own darkness; out of their darkness, they were seeking light. On and on, relentless and unflagging, the parade passed before my eyes. It was the tremendous procession of human aspiration, in its ceaseless march toward spirit.

My tale is nearly at an end. One day Uncle Sean called me into his little nest at the back of the shop to tell me that he had received from Viscount Gadarene a letter commending me in the highest possible terms for the quality of my work on the library at Teuchtershards. The receipt of this letter, he said, had finally persuaded him that the time had come to make a move which he had long had in mind. At the end of the year he would retire to his litle cottage at Cockburnspath, and he had determined to pass the business into the hands of wee Tam and myself as owners and partners on a basis of complete equality. He believed that we would make a splendid team, and was fully confident that he was leaving the fruits of forty years' labour and devotion in the safest and most capable hands.

So it was that a few months later the sign of 'Bookless and Bone' came down from above the little shop in Pitt Street, and that of 'Pagan and Tudhope' went up. We did consider whether 'Tudhope and Pagan' would be preferable, but we agreed in the end that 'Pagan and Tudhope' had a more confident ring to it. Wee Tam was married to Jenny-lass the following summer, and she still comes in to relieve him in the shop on two afternoons a week; and we get on extremely well together, all three of us.

So, after many tribulations, the mantle of contentment hangs me about. Yet sometimes, even now, the restless ghost of my dead dreams insinuates itself into my thoughts as I lovingly finger my dusty tomes, or pore over my accounts as my Uncle Sean did before me, in the little nest at the back of the shop. For Horatio Pagan, successful book dealer and respected citizen, seemed once to be singled out for a grimmer and more exacting destiny by far; and a tight, clenched knot of unfulfillment takes a grip, at times, of the centre of my gut. What I once was I shall always in some measure be; as the image of a woman once loved can still stir a ripple of longing on the calm sea of indifference, so the memory of my abandoned calling can yet arouse in me a poignant yearning. So if, in the uncertain gloaming of some dank November, a mysterious stranger were to appear at the door of Pagan and Tudhope in search of an elusive volume, I can never be certain that he would find the key turned against him in the lock.

CLAPPERTON

I

Clapperton woke agreeably one December morning in a bed warmed down the middle by the heat of his extended body, and stretched out his feet towards the cool peripheries. Something was not quite right. His right foot felt somehow not entirely normal. The cold sensation of the sheet upon his skin was in some obscure and inexpressible way different from that in the left foot. This fact had registered itself as a shadow upon his consciousness, a slight draught playing upon the warmth of his well-being, even before he was properly awake.

From the beginning Clapperton had felt his body as a burden to him. His earliest reading matter being the Bible, he would, a child of seven, fearfully peruse the thirteenth and fourteenth chapters of Leviticus and examine his person for the marks of leprosy. "And if, when the priest seeith it," he read, "behold, it be in sight lower than the skin, and the hair thereof is turned white, the priest shall pronounce him unclean: it is the plague of leprosy." The most miniscule pluke was thereafter an object of terror, and he was seldom without his magnifying glass, in those days. Suffering from headaches from the first, he imagined the interior of his skull sprouting, like that of Schumann, stalactites of knife-sharp bone. If he cut his finger or scratched his knee, every twinge in his back presaged for him (since he disbelieved in growing pains) the arching of his body in the rigid bow of tetanus. Nipped once in the elbow by a dog, for six months he felt compelled to swallow endless glasses of water to confirm that hydrophobia had not closed his throat, and to cast nervous glances at naked light bulbs to see if convulsions would follow. Often in the wee small hours he felt the buboes of plague rising in his groins and oxters.

As he grew older his terrors grew less dramatic, more muted, but no less hideous. Harmless moles thickened before his eyes into black cancer, mouth ulcers seemed the sloughing lesions of leukaemia, the buzzing of his ears heralded the imminent explosion of aneurysms in his brain. He became a furtive prowler in medical bookshops; if an assistant looked at him curiously, propped weak and sweating in a corner, he would casually flick over the pages to examine the price. During all these years he had been the victim of nothing more deadly than varicose veins. A policy of reassurance, said the doctor, and he was endlessly reassured; yet always, after a month or two of buoyancy, another symptom would appear. He understood his madness, appreciated his near-perfect health, yet each new fear seemed a tempting of fate: I am a hypochondriac, I know, he said, but it is not impossible, after all, for even a hypochondriac to be, for once genuinely ill... His hypochondria was thus to Clapperton as his boulder to Sisyphus, a world of eternally repetitive misery.

So the strange sensation in his foot broke in upon his optimism and his peace of mind that morning like a stealthy enemy. His mood when he had gone to rest the previous night had been unusually benign, for he had been full of unexampled hopes for the morrow. The kernel of these hopes lay in his having secured for the coming evening, after long and taxing efforts, a date with Trudy Otter, the girl across the street. This was sufficient of a landmark in Clapperton's existence to lighten more than a little the accustomed murk of his dealings with a hostile world, and to infect him with an uncharacteristic and general optimism. His waking, then, had been entirely pleasurable, for once he had felt eager to rise and capable of confronting with defiance the day's realities. The feeling in his foot, a suppressed buzzing now it seemed to him, was like a mild chastening of such unwarranted presumption and confidence, a reminder that, Trudy Otter or no, he walked still upon the earth and was subject to the trials of the flesh. It was far from enough, however, to prevent him leaping energetically of a sudden from his bed, in two swift movements throwing back the covers and shutting the window, and moving precipitately towards the bathroom.

Clapperton was a man of indeterminate age, of whom Crazy Jane might have found it hard to say whether he was an old man young, or a young man old. Suffice it to observe that his youth, though surviving, was not in its first flush. The most striking feature of his physical appearance was its lack of self-consistency. His body seemed countlessly fractured, and its component parts—as if held together by no unitary principle but rather by an act of will upon which no absolute reliance might be placed—appeared anxious to hive off in independent directions. His movements consequently tended towards the erratic. He now lolloped shivering down the passage and gathered up the mail from the floor.

Clapperton's eye fell at once upon an envelope addressed in threatening red typescript, and he knew the letter it contained to be one which he had been awaiting for some days with eagerness and apprehension. He was by profession a zoologist, and at that date suspended on half-pay from his post as director of a small private zoo, a glorified menagerie it might better be termed, specialising in ungulates, and controlled by a committee presided over by a splenetic individual named Colonel Menteith Dudgeon. For several months a venomous correspondence had been passing to and fro between Clapperton and Colonel Dudgeon, rich in libels, slanders and defamations of character, in assertions and counter-assertions, in threats and calumnies, in bluff talk of lawsuits and interim interdicts and veiled hints of blackmail. The specific origin of the differences between Clapperton and the committee was now obscured by the mists of time and overlaid by impenetrable accretions of argument, but the long and short of it lay in this, that Clapperton believed he was being ousted by Colonel Dudgeon because of the latter's inchoate resentment of his innate superiority, whereas Colonel Dudgeon believed that Clapperton was an impudent young coxcomb who was exceeding the limits of his responsibilities and must be taught to know his place. Objectively, all that need be said is that Clapperton's face simply did not fit with the committee. That it should not have fitted was not perhaps altogether outrageous, for it had to be admitted that it was a singularly odd one. Clapperton knew, at any rate, that he was in the right in these matters, but at times he was assailed by doubts of a metaphysical nature. Was he, for instance, in the scrupulously intelligent refutations he had penned to the bombastic outpourings of Colonel Dudgeon, guilty of the sin of intellectual pride? Was he not positively exulting in his rightness? Was his concern motivated by the love of truth, or by the dictates of an assertive will? Such were the considerations which lifted this episode from the level of a squalid and petty local squabble to realms of lofty and impersonal moral grandeur. But they are boring considerations and we shall pass them over. Enough to note that Clapperton's last letter, an effusion of nine and a half sides of foolscap, had been a model of uncompromising clarity and concision, countering undisciplined abuse with remorseless and unremitting logic, and that he was breathless to learn its effect.

Recalled to a sense of proportion however by the knowledge that tonight he was to be the escort of Trudy Otter, he contemptuously laid the letter aside until he had thoroughly washed himself, cleaned his teeth, and shaved selected areas of his face. Only then did he wrap himself in his dressing-gown and return to his bedroom to read the letter. It proved to be from Colonel Dudgeon's private secretary and read as follows:

Clapperton:

I write on behalf of Colonel Menteith Dudgeon who is confined to a couch of sickness. As you know, though doubtless do not care, he has been ailing for some time: his improvement had recently been such that we had entertained high hopes of his early recovery, but on receipt of your infamous letter he suffered a relapse and has now taken to his bed once more.

Clapperton! You are now dealing with a highly sensitive man; just how sensitive, perhaps only those who come into close and daily contact with him can realise. As for you, you are a noted misanthropist, anglophobe and *malade imaginaire*; your recent actions constitute a public scandal and fall not far short of criminal behaviour. You are a conceited and vain young fool and it would not surprise me to hear that you were guilty of self-abuse. Clapperton! If I were a man you would receive the thrashing you so richly deserve.

Edith Vole.

P.S. You are rotten in your soul.

Clapperton sat still upon the edge of his bed and gazed at this missive. His bedroom slipper seemed to be exerting an odd pressure upon the top of his right foot. He was at once outraged, vaguely amused, staggered at Miss Vole's immunity to logic, and nonplussed as to how to deal with such towering folly; but mainly he was hurt, deeply hurt, hurt to the quick and almost to the point of wanting to cry. Self-abuse! When he was seen walking down the streets with Trudy Otter resplendent upon his arm, they would see then whether he could be suspected of self-abuse. His face was red and his foot was buzzing. A blight had been cast upon his hopefulness and good humour.

He dressed quickly but meticulously in the raw cold of his bedroom, which was without a fire. That afternoon he would go to collect a small oil-heater which had long ago been promised him by his aged great-aunt. The visit was one which he had been postponing for weeks because of the considerable expenditure of his limited nervous resources which he knew that conversation with this old lady would involve. He reflected now that a price must be paid for everything enjoyed in this life, and that winter was approaching, and he began to prepare himself mentally for the ordeal ahead.

When he had dressed, Clapperton prepared and ate a light breakfast, his boiled egg exploding in the course of heating.

Boiled eggs, or rather about-to-be-boiled eggs, almost always did that to Clapperton; they appeared to harbour a grudge against him. Having washed up he walked for an inordinate time in circles around his small sitting-room and up and down the passage, thinking about Trudy Otter, and occasionally looking cautiously out of the window towards the residence of the Otters on the other side of the street. For some months past he had been visiting this admirable family regularly once a fortnight in order to deliver a political newsletter and to drink a cup of hot chocolate.

Clapperton never tired of contemplating the beauty of the domestic arrangements which prevailed in that estimable household. There was no direct communication whatever, verbal or otherwise, between Mr. Otter, a retired police sergeant of a chilling disposition, and his spouse. Their sense of each other's existence was registered instead by waves of palpable antipathy which passed to and fro from time to time between Mr. Otter's straight-backed chair in the window, where he sat sullenly playing solitaire or reading such sections of his newspaper as had a bearing on law and order, and the corner of the sofa at the opposite end of the room, facing the television, where reposed Mrs. Otter's weary limbs, the upper pair of which knitted compulsively throughout the evening. Such a wave of antipathy might be occasioned for instance by a vigorous rustle of the newspaper by Mr. Otter, by a click from his false teeth as he drained his coffee cup, or by one of his frequent full-chested coughs. Whenever Mrs. Otter spoke, to her son or daughter or to Clapperton, Mr. Otter would begin to shake his head in an ostentatious fashion and affect a supercilious smile, perhaps at the same time emitting a humourless laughing noise, a performance intended to convey his contempt for his wife's supposed inanity. If Mrs. Otter was watching television he would find occasion to go constantly in and out of the room in order to pass in front of her line of vision. The disruption of viewing which she suffered as a result of this behaviour was fully compensated for by the pleasure she derived from stonily ignoring it, staring expressionlessly ahead of her as if her husband were composed of thin air instead of all too solid flesh. The waves of antipathy were however very powerful at such times.

If Mr. Otter found it necessary to make reference to members of his family in the course of the few sentences he might speak to Clapperton, he would always refer to them collectively as "they", as if their individual personalities were submerged in the totality of a family unit which had its being in opposition to himself. Through Clapperton he could communicate to them without having to address them, which was useful. A certain hothouse quality could also be detected in the air around the area of the hearth, where the daughter Trudy was accustomed to sit at the feet of her brother Rex, but the cause of this lay not in the pleasures of hatred but in the pains of love, for their relationship was tragically incestuous. There existed in short in the Otter household an atmosphere which made Clapperton feel relaxed, confident and on top of the world.

The delectable Trudy spent these evenings flirting with Clapperton, but not of course out of any interest in his ridiculous person, but in order to induce a state of jealously in Rex, with whom she had always had a tiff. So she would sit close to her brother but looking away from him, looking always at Clapperton but removed from him by distance, and thus she would flirt with Clapperton. She spoke to him but her words were all for Rex. The latter always succeeded in appearing to ignore her, looking steadfastly in the opposite direction as he listened intently, and only from time to time making a vicious gibe at Clapperton. He, though seething within, never made any outward reaction to these gibes, preferring to leave Otter in doubt as to whether he had taken the point, whether the admirable shafts had reached home. Rex on his part, learning to anticipate this disappointing response, would betray by no indication that his remark had been intended as a shaft. Stalemate, then; but occasionally Rex's colossal fists would clench and unclench, and it was clear that he was contemplating the voluptuous pleasure he would derive from beating Clapperton's odd features into some semblance of order. Clapperton rather enjoyed the experience of being a sufficiently substantial person to arouse in another the desire to smash his face in; besides he had something of a daring nature, Clapperton, he liked to take risks, if they were gentle risks, risks which could be approached with caution.

His pleasure on these occasions would be tempered only by the presence of a Persian blue cat, vast and relentless, its eyes full of a dull and stubborn malice, which would invariably leap up on his lap where it would keep up an unremitting vigil, a torpid burden upon the meagre stirrings of Clapperton's manhood. Whenever he got up he experienced great difficulty in removing this animal, for it would dig its claws into his clothing and hang on for grim death; sometimes, indeed, the scene could be witnessed of Clapperton proceeding doubled up on his way out of the room, a huge cat suspended from his person, until he got out of the door, when he would dislodge it with a restrained blow from a paperweight, or a modified karate chop which he had developed specially for the purpose.

During the course of these repeated visits Clapperton had become gradually but heavily smitten with Trudy Otter, to the extent indeed that he believed himself to be in love. Perhaps he was not mistaken in this, for it would be wrong to suppose that, ridiculous though he was, Clapperton was incapable of love. The unworthy object of his desires was a honey blonde with a peaches-and-cream complexion and green eyes, of middle height and a figure good but well-covered, inclining very slightly to the fleshy, but not to an objectionable degree. Her conversation revealed her to be adequately sensitive but not overly intelligent. All of these qualities added up more or less to Clapperton's ideal of female desirability, for he was a conventional soul, Clapperton, in some respects. At first he had accepted that Trudy was bound to her brother Rex by unspeakable and indissoluble ties; a situation to which he had readily reconciled himself, for Clapperton always preferred his loves to be hopeless and inaccessible: that forestalled the possibility of disappointment. A week previously, however, the situation had changed decisively.

It happened thus. In the local grocer's shop one morning Clapperton found himself standing behind Trudy in a queue, and as she bought her wares he began to be incommoded by the attentions of the Otter family dog, a Shetland collie with a delicate pointed muzzle of great length, called John. John had previously been standing placidly behind Trudy, but on a sudden impulse he now began to nuzzle and prod at Clapperton's crotch with his long nose. Backing rapidly away in the face of these unwelcome attentions, by ill fortune he first stepped heavily on the toes of a woman standing behind him, causing her to cry out in a petulant but refined agony, and then, retreating still before the advancing muzzle, walked sideways into a huge pile of soup tins awaiting their disposal on the shelves, and brought them to earth with a mighty roar. In the ensuing mêlée Clapperton came into exciting physical contact with a Trudy contrite for the effects of her dog's excesses, and sympathetically anxious to help Clapperton survive his acute and bitter embarrassment; and somehow it came about that they left the shop in each other's company. Clapperton offered to carry Trudy's groceries for her, having a vague idea that this was the sort of thing a gentleman did for a lady; and the lady was grateful, needing both hands to control the unruly John, for whom Clapperton's crotch was still exerting a horrid fascination. At the door of the Otter house however the fickle creature deserted him in favour of the railings, enabling the two humans to stand for some moments exchanging pleasantries, which gradually degenerated on Clapperton's side into tortured incoherencies as he realised with terror that he was facing an unrivalled opportunity to ask Trudy for a date. Just as he was about to take flight in panic before this challenge, Trudy, who had that morning had a severe altercation with Rex, came to his aid by inviting herself to dinner with him the following Wednesday. "It would be better if you didn't pick me up here," she said without waiting for his acquiescence, "meet me at Scarlatti's at 7.30." This Clapperton took as a reference to Rex, so he indicated his compliance with a grateful gulp. As he turned to say goodbye while stepping off the pavement he unluckily knocked down a bicycle propped against the kerb, and then avoided by inches an ignominious death beneath the wheels of a passing milk-float.

The week since these events had passed for Clapperton in a turmoil of nervous apprehension. It must be explained that our hero's experience of the opposite sex was somewhat limited. Some months previously, feeling perhaps that life was passing him by, he had belatedly entered upon the sexual life by commencing visits to a brothel. He had had to come to an arrangement with the madam whereby he agreed to pay three times the normal charge, because of the inordinate time it took him to attain the conditions necessary for the successful achievement of coitus. Great was his envy of the petty businessmen who drove down to the brothel every evening after work, left their cars double-parked, and in cold weather sometimes even with the engines running, in, in and out, and out again, and home in time for tea.

Leaving aside these commercial amours, his only previous encounter had been with a large girl at a party many years before. She had followed him into a small study whither he had retreated for solitude, and seating herself beside him on a sofa engaged him in conversation. This proved a taxing experience since conversation was not Clapperton's long suit. Finding him unresponsive she had begun to insult and vilify him in indirect ways. Clapperton was insufficiently experienced in affairs of the heart to understand that the behaviour of this large female had its origin not in disgust with his person or personality, well-founded though such disgust might have been, but in resentment at the lack of interest which he was exhibiting in hers. Great then had been his surprise when in spite of all her insults her hand had come to rest upon his thigh.

Worse was to come. Feeling it incumbent upon him to make some token response to this potent gesture, Clapperton had advanced his face an inch or two closer to hers, and allowed the corners of his mouth to twitch enigmatically. On this slight prompting and without warning she had plunged her tongue into his mouth to a great depth, to the region of his tonsils, or where they would have been had he retained them. He was rather taken aback, but in spite of his surprise—for he was always a quick learner—had responded promptly, energetically, and in kind. Not that he derived any vestige of pleasure from the exercise. On the contrary, during the course of this and subsequent embraces he had taken care so as to position his head that he could, to relieve the boredom, study the titles of the books on the shelves opposite him, while his partner's eyes remained rapturously closed. Eventually he had taken advantage of a slight ebb in the tides of passion to excuse himself with the words, "All that beer", and departed never to return.

Restless and unsettled, Clapperton set off about midday for an early lunch. When he reached the public house he found that his favourite table was occupied by a group of English business executives. That it was occupied was bad enough, that it was occupied by a group of English business executives was beyond endurance. Small things like that had a profound effect upon Clapperton; they became symbols, fraught with baleful significance. A pall of gloom settled upon his spirit, a sort of end-of-the-world feeling. A claustrophobic sensation seized him, impelling him to be off and on his way. Viciously he attacked his bridie and swilled it down half-chewed with great gulps of beer. Then he stormed out of the pub and began walking away from the city centre towards the western suburbs where his great-aunt lived. Clapperton was at his best when walking. Not that he was a pleasant sight for the eyes of man while engaged in that activity, but within himself he was at his best. He walked very fast with great loose strides, outstripping all rivals, his head craning forward and his eyes bent on the ground, often half-tripping as he stubbed his toe against some irregularity of the pavement, but surging on regardless. Only while walking could Clapperton keep at bay the threats which from all sides impinged upon him, the swift motion absorbing the excesses of his inner energy. It was some four miles to his great-aunt's house but he covered the ground rapidly. As he walked the world once more brightened for him a little, though the day was cold, raw, and overcast. He thought of Trudy and looked ahead with pleasure. Even his foot seemed to have settled down; perhaps it was merely a circulatory disturbance, dispelled by exercise. For a time Clapperton even sang to himself a sonorous hymn tune. As he neared his destination however he had to suffer another affliction; a child who ran ahead of him then stopped, let him pass it then ran ahead again, and so on a great many times, until he thirsted for vengeance, and walked with fists clenched and grinding teeth.

At last Clapperton stood, ill at ease, at the front door of his great-aunt's door and rang the bell. There was no response, so he tried the handle: it turned, and he walked in. He had not taken two steps into the hallway before a Dutch bargedog called Trixie, a cross between a tailless black rat and an animated prune, launched itself snarling and with bared teeth at his ankles. Clapperton's large and flat foot met it in full career, and it described a shrieking parabola through the fetid air. Landing at the far end of the hall it fled screaming into the kitchen. Clapperton then looked into various rooms but found no one about, so he stood at the foot of the stairs and shouted his great-aunt's name, without conviction or much hope of a reply. Aunt Hetty was ninety-six years old, 85% blind, 95% deaf, semi-paralysed and limitlessly incontinent. Far from dumb however. Her daily needs were attended to by one Bairnsfather, a respectable man in late middle age. At this juncture, as Clapperton stood uncertain how to proceed, Bairnsfather appeared descending the stairs, and doing up his fly-buttons. "She's up the stair," he observed laconically, with a jerk of his thumb in that direction, and disappeared into the kitchen.

Clapperton went up and entered Aunt Hetty's bedroom, where he found her sitting swathed in rugs and shawls beside her bed, a sordid monument amid the tasteless bric-a-brac. She was unaware of his presence and he stood there for a few

moments observing her. She appeared to be in a state of sus-
pended animation, though her mouth made damp movements
from time to time, her dewlaps quivering peacefully. She
had smeared her face with powder which lay there in clotted
patches like flour. Clapperton did not like his great-aunt and
his great-aunt did not like Clapperton, whom she considered
an eccentric. All dealings and discourse with Aunt Hetty were
dominated by the fact of her age, to the extent that she had ceased
to be an individual and become a recalcitrant act of nature. It
was impossible to speak with her without being aware that she
was an old marvel, a living miracle, really wonderful, without
considerations of her extraordinary mental alertness, her extreme
touchiness, her indomitable will and so forth. Consequently she
was accustomed to getting away with murder. Clapperton found
her impossible to deal with, and now he had no idea how to
begin conversation with her.

"Hello!" he bellowed from a few feet away.

Several seconds later Aunt Hetty gave a start and looked blindly
in his direction. "Is that you, James?" she asked in a piercing
quaver. "I thought I heard Trixie give a wee squeak."

'No," Clapperton shouted back at her, "it's not James, it's
Thomas, it's your great-nephew Thomas Clapperton, and I have
come for the oil-heater which you so kindly promised me."

"Oh, it's you, Thomas," came her muted scream, "you never
come and see me."

Thinking of the oil-heater and of his neglect, Clapperton felt
it expedient to kiss her and he bent down, holding his breath.
When his hand took hold of her upper arm he felt through
the layers of shawl a loosely-hanging pouch of skin with no
flesh inside it. Kissing was not something which came easily to
Clapperton, even under the most propitious circumstances, and
these circumstances were not propitious. He aimed for a spot
on her cheek free from the clogged patches of powder, but she
turned her mouth to his and their moustaches mingled. Aunt
Hetty laughed a quavering and humourless laugh as Clapperton
extracted himself from this embrace.

"What have you come for?" she asked.

Clapperton was now well beyond the decencies of civilised discourse. "Oil-heater!" he shrieked.

Her sightless eyes shone with complacent malice.

"Oh, the oil-heater," she replied, "I'm afraid I've given it away. I didn't think you were coming, so I gave it to Bairnsfather. Have you met my man Bairnsfather? A wonderful man, terribly strong. He's a great big Highlander, you know, six-foot-four and very handsome."

The truth was that Bairnsfather was a Lowlander, a native in fact of Easthouses, Midlothian, five-foot-seven in height and unexceptional in features. Aunt Hetty's late husband, however, had been six-foot-one, moderately handsome and of distant Highland extraction. He remained her model of what a man should be, and, touchingly enough no doubt, she had recreated Bairnsfather in his image.

No oil-heater! Clapperton directed at his great-aunt a look of unadulterated hatred, and walked from the room without a word, fighting back the tears; distantly an angry peal of thunder rumbled, and outside large infrequent drops of rain began to splash on the pavement, for God had taken cognisance of Clapperton's discomfiture. He floundered down the stairs and through the hall, and rigid with rage and vexation began to stride down the garden path; the dog Trixie, who had ventured out to the front door, scuttled before him fouling the pathway in her terror, obliging Clapperton to stot gracelessly about the flagstones from foot to foot, sometimes so misjudging the distance that he landed, with a dull squelch, in that which he sought to avoid. In this manner he reached the garden gate and turned his face towards home.

So. Clapperton had the evening carefully planned. A leisurely aperitif or two, an intimate candlelit dinner at Scarlatti's, good conversation, a little courtly dalliance, perhaps a brandy orca kümmel with the coffee; and then they would proceed to the Foggos' party. That was what he was really picturing to himself: his entry into the Foggos' drawing-room with Trudy Otter on his arm, and then Carmen's face when she saw them. At one time, it must be explained, Clapperton had hoped to marry Carmen. Objectively speaking, of course, he had no conceivable justification for any such aspiration; but we can all hope, can we not? And in youth it is all hope, our lives are but dazzling mosaics of giddy imaginings.

Well, then ... that Carmen should have married someone else, that Clapperton could no doubt have accepted; but that she should have married Foghorn Foggo was beyond all endurance. But tonight, tonight she would appreciate what she had lost. She would understand, tonight, exactly what might have been. She would see him enter the room with Trudy Otter on his arm, her mouth would drop open just a little—not much, only a very little—perhaps her colour might change almost imperceptibly. She would fix him long and hard with her grey-blue eyes, she would hold out her elegant hand in greeting: then she would glance to her left and see Foggo, see the infamous and vulgar Foghorn ogling *his* young lady, and a wave of blank despair would surge up in her soul...

Inflated with such conjectures, at twenty-five past seven sharp Clapperton arrived scrubbed, shaven and smartly dressed at Scarlatti's Italian restaurant. He was nervous, but in full control of his faculties. He entered the cocktail bar, ordered a medium sherry, and settled himself comfortably to wait. At twenty-five to eight he looked at his watch. He knew that it was a lady's prerogative to be late. At twenty to eight he bought himself another sherry, and as its level dropped and no Trudy appeared his nervousness increased and he began to cross and uncross his legs too frequently and to peer anxiously at the door every time someone came in. He endeavoured however to maintain a casual pose for the benefit of the barman, before whom he was beginning to feel conspicuous. He did not want to buy another sherry before Trudy arrived, but his apprehension was making him drink faster than usual. At three minutes to eight he got up and went outside, and gazed up and down the street for some time. No Trudy Otter hove into sight. Then he went back to the bar and bought a third sherry. By five past eight the idea was establishing itself in his mind that he had been stood up, and at ten past he knew for certain that Trudy would not come. With this realisation his agitation began to leave him: things were returning to normal. Nevertheless he continued to wait on, reluctant to admit that it was all over, anxious to give Trudy every chance, determined that it should never be said that he had deserted his post. At eight-fifteen, however, he rose. Clapperton was not prepared to wait that length of time for anyone, certainly not for someone as fat as Trudy Otter.

Clapperton entered the restaurant and stood in painful embarrassment within the doorway, waiting to be shown to his table. He would have preferred, because of the obscenity of his head, to have been invisible, for the previous day he had had his hair cut. Clapperton was really satisfied with the state of his hair only for brief periods of ten days or so midway between haircuts, which took place at roughly monthly intervals. For any marked departure in either direction from the optimum desirable hair-length rendered his head obscene, in Clapperton's opinion. Could he not then have had his hair cut strictly to this optimum length, rather than shorter? No, because that would have necessitated its being cut more frequently, at fortnightly rather than monthly intervals, which would have been insupportable to him. Besides which it is almost impossible, if a short styling is desired, to persuade a barber not to crop the back of the neck; and in Clapperton's view the faculty of barbering, in a barber, came second, though a close second, to the faculty of silence. And in this world you can never have everything. Thus it was that always after a haircut Clapperton was for a time reluctant to exhibit the state of his head in public, until the passage of days had mitigated to some degree its obscenity.

A waiter at last appeared and Clapperton gave his name. The waiter however had difficulty in understanding it.

"Ah, yes, two sir, no?" he said at last, after consulting his book.

"One now," Clapperton replied rudely, and suffered the grim

journey to his solitary table with set jaw and downcast eyes. He ordered Schnitzel Holstein and a bottle of Beaujolais, and as he waited the humiliation of his position began to stab at him. His first reaction to his jilting had been one of relief, as if he had been released from a taxing obligation, but Clapperton was not a man to be satisfied for long. It came upon him that once more he was alone, that he was the only lone diner in the restaurant, that most of the others indeed were couples, young couples in the main. His table was of course set for two, and it seemed to him that all the other diners had noticed this and were talking about him in whispers and giggles, making obscene cracks about him from behind their hands.

So rather than have to look upon the humanity assembled around him and suffer their insolent gaze in return, in a desperate attempt to seclude himself he drew from his pocket the letter from Edith Vole, and perused it with bitter distaste. Its ringing, confident phrases clanged in his ear, taunting him and vilifying him. "You are a conceited and vain young fool and it would not surprise me to hear that you were guilty of self-abuse." Every time he looked up some commonplace young man was leering towards him and whispering to his companion that Clapperton was a conceited and vain young fool who looked as if he were guilty of self-abuse, but not to look now, and after gazing with sheep's eyes at her lover the girl would crane her neck round adroitly towards Clapperton and quickly turn away again with a smothered snigger to her lover's eyes. Clapperton felt a profound hatred stir within him for the whole race of women.

Inflamed with anger and distress he fell to eating Schnitzel Holstein with voracious appetite and to swilling red wine at a high speed. His foot had begun buzzing again. As he ate he was made aware of the obtrusive presence, at a table a little distance to his left, of an Englishman. This yapping, yelping creature was making himself heard at no inconsiderable distance in giving an account to his party of guests of the events of his Highland tour. It was perhaps inevitable that the sum of Clapperton's pain, anger and annoyance should be gathered together into a pure and single hatred of this innocent and inoffensive personage, who remained oblivious of the emotion he was arousing even when Clapperton, having finished eating and being sufficiently drunk, swung his chair round to face him, and resting his elbow on the table and his chin on his hand, concentrated upon him a look of relentless malice.

What Clapperton stood in need of at this juncture was the restraining influence of a little woman, who would soothe him and ridicule him and cause him to regain a sense of proportion, perhaps even place a cooling hand on his brow and so on. Yet even should such a creature exist, and be sitting there, would Clapperton have been able to put up with her, or she with Clapperton? Probably not. However that is by the way, and irrelevant, for Clapperton's only companion at this restaurant table was the hunch of bitterness within his breast, the hunch of endless longing and repeated failure and indescribable folly, suddenly rendered insupportable by the mindless yelping on his left. Accordingly, when he heard the phrase "...and then we caime to a little plaice called Arrow-tchah," he felt impelled to rise to his feet. By ill chance the table-cloth became entangled between his knees, and the wine bottle fell to the floor, but he pressed on regardless and soon found himself standing by the Englishman's table and enunciating rather distantly these sentiments:—

"I wish you to know that I detest and despise you. I do not propose to go into the rights and wrongs, the why's and wherefore's, I am in no condition to do that; but I wish to make it abundantly clear to you that your presence here is a matter of offence to me."

The man gaped at him without pain or comprehension; one or two of his companions emitted injured gasps; a waiter approached. A brief silence ensued, of which Clapperton could envisage no satisfactory break, so he moved with dimmed consciousness towards the door, scattering waitresses like chaff before him in his passage. He was about to plunge into the street when a hand fell on his shoulder. It was the head waiter, advising him that he had neglected to pay the bill. Clapperton looked at it vaguely, drew a number of notes from his wallet and handed them over. Then he walked out, leaving behind him a tip of some forty per cent.

Rage and shame in his heart, he made his way through the damp, foggy streets to the suburban flat of Stuart and Carmen Foggo. Trudy or no Trudy, he would show them, somehow, that he was not a person to be trifled with. When he arrived the little party was already in full swing. Just a few people, a dozen or so, not more, had been invited to meet Stuart and Carmen again. Stuart and Carmen were up for Christmas, up from London, where Stuart had been a merchant banker for the past six years. They had, of course, retained an Edinburgh residence—that, Clapperton thought, was typical. He knew only two other people present, namely his cousin and his cousin's wife: he no longer moved in such circles. Carmen greeted him warmly enough and said at once that they must have a long chat. Half an hour passed, however, then an hour, and the long chat had still not materialised. Carmen was now over by the fire on the far side of the room, in animated conversation with two or three young men, smoking incessantly, laughing every now and again that pealing, almost plangent laugh which never failed to assert its power over him. Edged into a corner by the door, no longer making any attempt to enter into the conversation of those around him, Clapperton watched her as she drank, her long slender fingers curled around the stem of her glass. When she glanced his way for a moment her eyes had a glassy, preoccupied look, and they flicked quickly away again.

Stuart's voice sounded above the other voices in the room, the words undifferentiated but the bray overriding. He could not pronounce his *R*'s properly and for that reason exaggerated his drawl, in the hope that people would mistake this incapacity for affectation. Many did. He had patronised Clapperton when they had met on the latter's arrival, there was no room for doubt about that, and it rankled. Clapperton was determined not to let him get away with it, but time was passing and he was at a loss to think of a way to get even. Yes, time was short—only a moment or two before, Stuart had shown the first departures to the door. Not of course that Clapperton thought of him as Stuart. Foggo was his surname; "Foghorn Foggo" they had called him at school, and this epithet described him more than adequately. Clapperton put down his glass and made his way to the cloakroom.

He stood for a moment looking at himself in the mirror, with distaste. It seemed to him that his face looked bloated, as if his collar were too tight. He padded up and down gloomily for a little, hands in pockets, sunk in thought. The air was redolent with Foggo's cigar.

Clapperton stood still and looked around him. The men's coats were hanging lumpishly from the too few pegs, one on top of the other. Checking nervously to make certain that his own coat was still there—for one can never be too sure—he found his hand entering by chance the useful inside pocket located in the lining, where he kept his wallet. A thought occurred to him, and he looked about him again. In a corner stood a tall, solid brass umbrella stand. Withdrawing his wallet, Clapperton checked its contents, then after a moment's consideration laid it carefully on the floor between the umbrella stand and the wall, well into the shadow. He stood back and studied it: it was not easily visible, but from a certain angle the metal reinforcement on one corner glinted slightly. Not daring for an instant to examine his impulse more closely, he adjusted his tie, breathed deeply and returned immediately to the party. He walked straight up to Foggo, who smiled blandly and good-naturedly.

"Ah, Tom, we haven't had a chance..."

"Return my wallet to me, Foggo," said Clapperton quietly with controlled emotion, "and we'll agree to forget it." Only his cousin's wife, who had been talking to Foggo, heard what was said.

Foggo appeared genuinely puzzled. "Come again?" he faltered.

"I think you understand me, Foggo," said Clapperton more

loudly, and very distinctly. "If you give me back my property it will go no further." This time Carmen had heard without a doubt—Clapperton could see from the corner of his eye that she had stiffened, and imagined with satisfaction the sudden falling-off of her interest in the young men; but she was too proud to turn her head.

"I take it you're not serious, Tom," said Foggo, gathering himself together and retrieving his *sang-froid*, "but I think you've a funny idea of a joke."

"Yes, what on earth is all this about, Tom," asked Isobel, the cousin's wife, her laughter shaking with unease.

"It's about this, Isobel," said Clapperton, his temper rising. "This man has purloined my wallet, and I want it back."

"Oh, this is ridiculous!" gasped Foggo, now very white. His *r* was not quite a *w*, rather something between and *w* and a French *r*, but closer to the former. By this time everyone in the room was aware that something was happening.

"Oh, this is widiculous!" yelled Clapperton, now quite beside himself. "Foghorn Foggo, Foghorn Foggo!" he brayed in jeering mimicry, like a child.

His cousin, who appeared to feel responsible for him, stared at his shoes in helpless embarrassment, but Isobel pluckily endeavoured to come to terms with the horror of it.

"What possible reason can you have for making such an accusation, Tom?" she pleaded with Clapperton.

"I shall try to keep calm," he replied. "My wallet was in the inside of my overcoat fifteen minutes ago. It is no longer there. I have been standing beside the door, and since that time only one person has left this room—Stuart Foggo. I hope I make myself plain."

"How much was in your wallet, Tom?" asked Carmen coolly, her velvety voice cutting.

Clapperton turned to her with a face of ice. "Seven pounds," he replied. "One Bank of Scotland five pound note, one Royal Bank of Scotland pound note, one Bank of England pound coin. Also my banker's card."

She threw back her head and let out a long, slightly hysterical peal of laughter. "And you really think that Stuart needs your seven pounds?"

"Oh, clever, clever," Clapperton grimaced, snarling with malice. "But they say that with some people, the more they get the more they want... Search him! Search him!" he bellowed suddenly. "Hold his arms!" And he made a dive at a side-pocket of Foggo's jacket.

"Whoa! Whoa there!" cried Clapperton's cousin, galvanised into action and leaping between them. "This is getting beyond a joke!"

"Its outwageous!" shouted Foggo.

"Outwageous! Outwageous! Foghorn Foggo!" bawled Clapperton, foaming at the mouth. There was universal consternation.

"May I try to introduce an element of sanity into the proceedings?" asked a demure young lady, stepping foward. "Before searching Stuart, might it not be an idea to search the house in case Mr. Clapperton has *mislaid* his wallet?"

"I'm agreeable," said Clapperton promptly, folding his arms, staring up at the ceiling and whistling affectedly under his breath. "Search away."

He remained in the room, striding up and down, while the others went out to search the passage and cloakroom; at first Foggo also remained sitting on the sofa with his head in his hands staring at the floor, visibly upset; but soon he too got up and went out without looking at Clapperton. Clapperton could hear the excited, low-toned voices buzzing away as the hunt went on, and presently the inevitable whoop of feminine triumph as the missing object was retrieved. It was inevitable, too, that it was Carmen who led the way back into the room, a fixed smile of heartless triumph splitting her face in two.

"Could this be yours?" she asked quietly, holding the wallet up between finger and thumb. Foggo was standing beside her, the tears rolling softly down his cheeks.

"I thought he was a fwiend," he muttered brokenly.

Clapperton turned aside, his face suffused with shame.

"Your husband might have dropped it out there himself just now," he stammered, as lamely and unconvincingly as possible.

At this a general moan, a kind of suppressed, mirthless guffaw arose from the entire company. Carmen cast the wallet at his feet without a word.

"It's unbelievable," said somebody. Clapperton was aware of their hostile faces gazing at him now with undisguised contempt.

"Oh, God!" he said, taking a step forward, stopping, closing his eyes and making a gesture as if to wave reality away from before him. "I've made a terrible mistake, a dreadful, disgraceful mistake. God forgive me." He dropped to his knees before Carmen and bowed his head to the ground. "Oh, God, the shame, the shame! Friends, I feel like disappearing beneath the floor. Oh, God, the shame!"

"Huh!" the same voice made itself heard.

Clapperton rose slowly to one knee and then to his feet. Bravely, but with dread, he looked around the company. With Carmen at their head and setting the tone, they were united in implacability. He bent again, picked up his wallet and put it in his pocket. Then an idea seemed to occur to him, he took it out again and impulsively held it out towards Foggo.

"Take it, Stuart—it's yours—it's the least I can do to make amends..."

Foggo let out a terrible sound, a sob contorted with hideous laughter, and waving him away with his left hand buried his face on Carmen's shoulder. Clapperton sighed deeply, nodding his head as if in acknowledgement of the justice of Foggo's reaction.

"Friends, I've ruined the party for all of you," he said simply. "Stuart, I've wronged a better man than myself. I can't ask you to forgive me, only God can do that. Please just let me go."

With that he began to grope his way towards the door, and the crowd parted silently to let him pass. Someone spat on the floor. Shoulders hunched and head bowed, Clapperton went straight out of the front door, down the garden path and onto the street. He was breathing fast, sweating profusely and his knees were shaking with a violent tremor.

"I've done it! I've done it!" he whispered to himself with joy. "What a humiliation! What a magnificent, astonishing humiliation! And in front of Carmen! Oh, to make myself do that, in front of Carmen, to carry it through, to stoop so low, I never believed I could do it! Oh, what glory!"

Soon he could no longer contain his excitement: he had to stop, and gripping hold of a lamp-post with both hands, he went into a kind of orgasm.

He stretched himself up slowly to his full height, and a great sigh, a weary, spent sigh issued from the depths of him. Instantly his exaltation left him and a real shame, cold, clammy and all-pervasive, swept through his soul, and with it a sense of utter futility. He began to walk slowly on down the foggy street, in the raw, dank air, heavy as lead with fatigue. After a time his shame brought him to a halt. They would be talking about him back there even now, discussing with glee the extraordinary exhibition he had made of himself; Carmen by this time would be putting in a good word for him, saying that he must be under stress, that he was a very nice, kind chap in many ways, but odd, odd; heads would be nodding sagely, some would be barely hiding their smiles ... he realised that he had left his coat behind. He must go back. Yes, he could not leave things the way they were, he would go back and put things right somehow, the coat would be his excuse.

Clapperton returned back along the row of terraced houses, mocked as he went by lighted Christmas trees. He crept up the path, and from behind the gaily-coloured curtain of the front room, lit up from within, he could hear their laughter. He stole up to the window and he heard it louder, their relieved, exuberant mirth, their inextinguishable laughter at himself and his ludicrous, shameful performance. He rang the bell and waited. At length the door was opened by his cousin, the overcoat on his arm.

"Yes, you forgot your coat," he said coldly, holding it out.

Clapperton took it but came on over the threshold, pushing past his cousin who offered no resistance. His eyes blinking against the light, he made his way once more into the drawing-room and paused wearily in the doorway. The guests had heard the bell and knew it was he; they seemed expectant, and at his appearance conversation was instantly silenced.

"I just wanted you all to know," said Clapperton haltingly, holding his coat, "that I am not quite such a fool as I appear to be." He spoke with great sincerity. "The whole thing was a practical joke—an ill-judged one, I admit, but nevertheless only a joke." He hesitated, hoping for a response, but no one spoke; he saw that he had made a deplorable impression. Prominent before his eyes was the face of Foggo, utterly expressionless. Carmen, however, was close to tears, chewing her lower lip and staring at the wall. "That's all I wanted to say," blurted Clapperton, and turned to go.

As he did so, he heard that same malicious voice. "It may not have been much of a joke," it said clearly, "but it was certainly practical!" A loud gust of tension-dispelling laughter rewarded these words.

In the hallway Clapperton found that Isobel, his cousin's wife, had followed him out, and his eyes filled with tears of gratitude for this act of kindness. He turned to say a word of thanks, and as he did so by ill fortune he tripped heavily over the cord of an electric radiator, and stumbled on into the outer lobby. Not looking back, he made his way into the street and set off aimlessly through the cold patchy fog. But he had no idea where he was heading, and soon he drifted to a halt and stood there vacantly, unaware of where he was or what he was doing. Three youths overtook him, talking loudly, and when they had passed they kept turning round every few paces to walk backwards staring at him standing there alone in the middle of the pavement. Eventually this mindless behaviour twisted his soul into uncontrollable fury. He threw his overcoat on the pavement and stamped his foot in rage.

"This is widiculous!" he screamed at them, the sounds of his hysteria echoing strangely fog-muffled through the calm of the suburb. "This is outwageous! Foghorn Foggo! Foghorn Foggo! Foghorn Foggo!"

It was some time before Clapperton came fully to himself and began slowly to make his way home once more, moaning gently to himself as he drifted alone through the now deserted streets. When eventually he reached his small flat he spent some time meticulously re-arranging certain of his books on their shelves. It was bitterly cold, and he was without an oil-heater. Nonetheless he began slowly to undress, arranging his clothes with great care on a chair, brushed his suit and hung it away, brushed and polished his shoes. Then he washed with great thoroughness, brushed his teeth and brushed his hair, moaning all the while. Some time in the early hours he found himself once more in the bed from which he had arisen the previous morning with such sturdy hopes.

When a person weeps while lying flat on the back the tears do not descend down the front of the cheeks on either side of the nose, as might be supposed, but course sideways down into the ears. Thus it was that when sleep at last overtook Clapperton it found him with the cavities of his ears generously filled with salt tears, which he had not had the heart to mop away, for they seemed to sympathise with him and comfort him a little in his distress. Yet in the morning when a weak ray of sunshine alighted upon the waking Clapperton, it seemed the reflection of a meagre hope which stirred once more within his heart. Perhaps Trudy had been unavoidably detained somewhere, and even in a moment the phone would ring with her contrite apologies ... Or Carmen, it might be, in an hour or two would call round, pathetically anxious to make amends for her unworthy misapprehension of his motives ... The previous night it had seemed to Clapperton that life might strike him down; but life could never strike him down, for it had never raised him up, and it never would raise him up, never. So Clapperton arose, meagrely sustained by this wretched hope, not briskly but resolutely enough, to live another day.